the shopping websites

Zingin.com

Prentice Hall

An Imprint of Pearson Education

London New York Toronto Sydney Tokyo
Singapore Madrid Mexico City Munich Paris

PEARSON EDUCATION LIMITED

Head Office:
Edinburgh Gate
Harlow
Essex CM20 2JE
Tel: +44 (0)1279 623623
Fax: +44 (0)1279 431059

London Office:
128 Long Acre
London WC2E 9AN
Tel: +44 (0)20 7447 2000
Fax: +44 (0)20 7240 5771

First published in Great Britain in 2000

© Paul Carr 2000

ISBN 0-130-40937-5

The right of Paul Carr to be identified as author of
this work has been asserted by it in accordance with the
Copyright, Designs and Patents Act 1988.

British Library Cataloguing-in-Publication Data
A catalogue record for this book can be obtained from the British Library.

All rights reserved; no part of this publication may be reproduced, stored in a retrieval system, or transmitted, in any form, or by any means, electronic, mechanical, photocopying, recording or otherwise, without prior written permission from the Publisher.

Many of the designations used by manufacturers and sellers to distinguish their products are claimed as trademarks. Pearson Education Limited has made every attempt to supply trademark information about manufacturers and their products mentioned in this book.

10 9 8 7 6 5 4 3 2 1

Typeset by Land & Unwin (Data Sciences) Ltd
Printed and bound by Ashford Colour Press, Gosport, Hampshire

The publisher's policy is to use paper manufactured from sustainable forests.

contents

Introduction v

1 The internet: a (very) brief guide 1

2 Directories and department stores 12

3 Entertainment 22

4 Computers and technology 38

5 Clothing and fashion 52

6 Health and beauty 62

7 Sports and outdoor 68

8 Home and garden 76

9 Food and drink 81

10 Events and tickets 89

11 Travel 92

12 Toys and gifts 98

13 Classifieds and auctions 106

Quick reference guide 112

While the publisher and author have made every effort to ensure that all entries were correct when this book went to press, the Internet moves so quickly that there may now be website addresses that don't work, or new sites we should cover. If you encounter any incorrect entries when using the book, please send us an email at **oops@zingin.com** *and we will make sure it is dealt with in the next edition.*

The publisher and author can accept no responsibility for any loss or inconvenience sustained by the reader as a result of the content of this book.

introduction

Welcome to the world's biggest department store!

No matter whether you're buying your weekly food shopping or a gift for the person who has everything, the internet contains thousands of shops offering millions of products – and they're all just a mouse click away.

Finding ways to spend money online is not difficult. You only have to switch on the TV or open a magazine to be bombarded with adverts for sites that claim to offer 'unbelievable value' and 'hassle-free shopping' but how do you know which ones offer the best products at the lowest prices? Well … that's where we come in.

When we decided to put this book together we were determined not to create just another long directory of shopping sites – there's plenty of those already and most only add to the confusion. Instead, we've tried to stick to the principles we use when selecting sites for Zingin.com, our online web guide – if a shop is the best of the bunch, you'll find it here – if it's not, you won't.

So who is this book written for? Well, if you've never bought anything online and don't want to get ripped off or if you're a net-shopaholic who wants to find the best bargains then it's for you. All of the shops listed are well established and offer the best value and levels of service to UK shoppers so you can shop with confidence, knowing that you're in safe hands.

We've tried to make it as easy as possible for you just to dive in and get started with the book. The chapters have been put in a (hopefully) logical order, starting with sites that help you find shops and compare prices, then retailers that specialise in certain types of products (entertainment, travel, clothing, gifts etc.) and finally auction and classified services which allow you to sell your own unwanted items online.

Although only the very best of the web has made it into these pages, we've headed up each section with **the best of the best** so you don't have to waste any time getting started and, if you know the name of the site you want, you can look it up in the quick reference section tucked away neatly at the back.

With the help of this book it should be pretty straightforward to find the products or services you're looking for but if you do have any problems please come and visit us on the web (**www.zingin.com**) and we'll try our best to help you out.

Happy shopping!

Paul Carr
Founder
Zingin.com

the internet: a (very) brief guide

The fact that you've bought this book means that you've probably used the internet before, either at home or at work. If, however, you're still getting to grips with the basics then read on for the answers to some of our most frequently asked questions.

Getting started

There are plenty of online resources to help you get the most out of the web but none of them are any use if you're not online. By far the quickest way to get started is to pop into your local newsagent or computer shop and get hold of one of the zillions of free internet access CDs stuck to the front of popular computer magazines. However, if you want a bit more information before taking the plunge have a quick look at the following pointers.

I'm new to the internet, how do I get started?

It goes without saying that to take advantage of the information contained in this book, you'll need access to the internet. If you want to connect from home you'll need a computer (a 486 or above should be fine), a modem (new computers usually come with one built in) and a spare telephone socket within easy reach of the computer.

The modem, which plugs in to the back of your computer (unless it's already built in) and then into the telephone socket, has basically one purpose – to allow your computer to send and receive data over a telephone line. Once you're plugged in, all that remains now is to decide which internet service provider (ISP) you will use to connect to the 'net. Your ISP provides a gateway to the internet and when you ask your computer to connect to the web or to send and receive e-mails, your modem is actually dialling into their network which, in turn, is connected to the rest of the internet. This explains how you can send an e-mail to Egypt or to Edinburgh for the same price – you're only paying for the call to the ISP (the price of a local call or less). If you don't want to connect from home then most large libraries provide free or low-cost internet access and there are plenty of internet cafés around the country who will be happy to help you take your first online steps.

Which ISP is right for me?

Choosing an ISP can be a complicated business with some companies offering free access, some offering free telephone calls and a few still clinging on to monthly charges – all trying to persuade you that you'll get a better deal with them. Pretty confusing. Basically, the right ISP for you will depend on what you want to use the internet for.

If you're only interested in e-mail, surfing the web and maybe building a personal website then you'll be fine with a free service. Of course, there's no such thing as a free lunch and you'll usually still have to pay either local call charges or a fixed fee for unlimited access. Luckily for internet users, there's fierce competition between ISPs and you can find some excellent deals if you shop around. To get online with a free service you can either pick up a connection CD from one of the high street shops who have set up their own ISPs (WHSmiths, PC World, Waterstones and Tesco to name just a few) or call up one of the providers advertised in any of the popular internet magazines.

If you want to use the internet for business and require extra features such as high speed access, a business website or your own domain name (e.g. you@yourname.com) then you'll need use a specialist ISP who will usually charge a monthly fee in addition to your normal phone charges.

If you already have internet access at work, university, school or in a local internet café then surf over to ISP Review (www.ispreview.co.uk) for a full run-down of the best and worst UK internet service providers.

Online help and advice

Ok, so you've made it online and you're looking for help and advice on how to get the most out of the web? Of course, to find the best websites to get you started you'll want to take a quick trip to your friends at Zingin.com (**www.zingin.com**) but for technical support and general advice, try these.

Why does it say that the page I'm looking for is not found?

The internet is in a constant state of development and things are getting moved around and deleted all the time. Anyone who's spent more than a couple of minutes on the web will have clicked on a link or typed in a web address only to get hit with the dreaded 'File not found' message. If the page you're looking for seems to have vanished, the most likely cause is that the page has been deleted or moved to another address. If an address doesn't work, try removing bits from the end until you find something. For example; if the address **www.asite.com/directory/files/filename.html** produces an error, try deleting the 'filename.html' bit to see if there's anything at **www.asite.com/directory/files**. If you're still getting an error then try **www.asite.com/directory** and finally **www.asite.com**. If you run out of things to delete and still can't find the site then it's probably temporarily unavailable or has been deleted. Sites that have been moved can often be tracked down using a search engine such as Google (**www.google.com**) – simply type in the name of the page/site and see what comes up.

What is the best software for browsing the web?

Most of the free ISPs include a copy of Microsoft Internet Explorer on their access disks and, unless you really want to, there's no real need to use another browser. If you do fancy a change or want to fight back against Microsoft's quest for world domination, there are some alternatives worth trying. The best of the bunch is Netscape Navigator which contains a very similar range of features to Internet Explorer but with slightly less polish. The best way to describe Netscape is like Burger King to Microsoft's McDonald's – try them both and decide which one tastes better. Other choices can be found at **www.browserwatch.com**.

How can I find out more about using the web?

The internet used to be controlled by academics, scientists and computer geeks and unless you knew your way around it could be very scary indeed. In cyberspace no one could hear you scream. Nowadays, using e-mail and surfing the web is like driving a car – pretty straightforward when you get the hang of it even if you don't know exactly what's going on under the bonnet. Having said that, if you want to get the most out of your internet experience you'll need to get a basic grasp of the way it works. One of the best guides to how the 'net works and what it can do is Learn the Net (**www.learnthenet.com**) which contains some very well-written tutorials covering e-mail, downloading files, building a website and plenty of other useful stuff. If you're baffled by internet jargon you'll definitely want to have a quick look at PC Webopedia (**www.pcwebopedia.com**) and for beginner's advice with a UK perspective surf over to BBC Webwise (**www.bbc.co.uk/webwise**).

Buying online

Throughout this book you'll find sites that allow you to order products, book tickets and generally spend your hard-earned cash. The first thing to remember is that using your credit card online is 100% safe providing you take a few sensible precautions.

How do I know which companies to trust?

Firstly, wherever possible stick to companies you've heard of. If someone you know has bought from a particular site without any problems or if it's a household name then the risk is greatly reduced.

As with any purchase on or off the web, you should always ensure that you are buying from a reputable company. Sites such as Amazon (www.amazon.co.uk) and Last Minute (www.lastminute.com) are very well-known internet traders and so are a risk-free option but if you do want to order from a company you've never heard of then take a look at the next few questions which will hopefully address your concerns.

Can hackers get hold of my credit card number once I've typed it in?

As long as you only type your credit card details into sites that offer encryption security (SSL), your information will be perfectly safe. Look for a yellow padlock on the bottom right of your browser window if you are using Internet

Explorer or, in Netscape, look for a closed padlock. This ensures that information sent to the site is encrypted and so cannot be intercepted by hackers. If the site is not secure, be very wary about placing an online order and *never* send credit card information via normal e-mail.

How can I check on the status of my order?

Many larger sites offer order tracking facilities which allow you to check the progress of your order until it is delivered. If there is no order tracking, ensure there is a contact telephone number in case you need to chase things up.

Is it safe to order from outside the UK?

Orders placed with companies outside the UK are not protected by UK sale of goods or safety legislation. Only order from abroad if you know and trust the company you are dealing with and even then, try to stick within Western Europe and the USA.

Am I going to get stung by hidden costs?

There's no 'internet tax' for orders made online but as with any mail order purchase you should always check whether your order includes postage and packing costs. Also, remember that orders from outside the UK may be subject to additional customs and import costs.

Is there a regulatory body for online traders?

The Consumers Association have been looking after the interests of shoppers for years and have recently launched a scheme to protect you on the web. The Which? Webtrader scheme (**www.which.net/webtrader**) requires its members to abide by a strict code of conduct if they want to join. Sites that have the Webtrader logo have to provide a decent level of service otherwise Which? will simply kick them out! It's worth remembering that membership of the scheme isn't compulsory and many reputable businesses are not members, so if you don't see the logo don't assume the worst, but if you do – expect the best.

What if the goods don't arrive or my credit card is used fraudulently?

Don't panic if products ordered online take a while to arrive. Just like in the real world, delays do happen and things can be out of stock – even if you receive a confirmation saying that everything is fine. However, if you've waited longer than 21 days then you should contact the company concerned to hurry them up.

A gentle reminder will usually be enough to get things moving but if you're still not getting anywhere you should contact your credit card issuer for advice. If the site is a member of the Which? Webtrader scheme, make sure you let them know as well.

If you have problems with an order made using a credit card, you will usually be able to recover any lost money from your card issuer. If you're concerned about fraud, call your credit card company to check their policy regarding fraudulent transactions.

Can I buy anything I like over the web?

Yes and no. Yes, most things are available – from sweets and cakes to cars and houses but, no, you can't necessarily order them from the UK. The law on ordering from abroad using the internet is the same as using the phone and there are certain products which it is illegal to bring into the country. Some good examples of this are: drugs, certain food items, adult material, pets and automatic weapons. You can probably guess the law's position on drugs and guns but if you need to check out what is allowed, visit Customs and Excise (www.hmce.gov.uk).

For the full low-down on internet shopping, check out www.zingin.com/guide/shopping.

Searching the web

Finding what you're looking for on the internet can be like trying to find a very small needle in a very large haystack. Search engines are fine if you're looking for very specialist information (the population of Peru or the Belgian translation of *Romeo and Juliet*) but when it comes to popular subjects like travel or music it's easy to get swamped by the number of sites available.

So how do you find the information you need without wading through pages of irrelevant junk? Good question.

What is the best search engine?

That all depends on what you're looking for. There are literally thousands of search engines and directory sites and each has its own strengths and weaknesses.

For general searches we recommend Google (www.google.com) which ranks sites on both relevance and popularity (how many other sites link to them). You'll usually find the information you want on the first page of results but if you have no success, try the same search on Hotbot (**www.hotbot.com**) and Altavista (**www.altavista.co.uk**).

If you are looking for UK-specific information there are plenty of home-grown search engines which should fit the bill. A couple of our favourites are UK Plus (**www.ukplus.co.uk**) and Search UK (**www.searchuk.co.uk**).

How do I find a business or service?

Looking for a plumber? An electrician? A four-star hotel in Derby? Rather than reaching for the *Yellow Pages*, take a wander over to Scoot (**www.scoot.co.uk**) which will let you search by business type, location or the name of the company you need. If you prefer to use good old *Yellow Pages* then it can be found at Yell (**www.yell.com**).

Is it really possible to get free software over the internet? Where can I find it?

The internet is full of free software, much of which can be downloaded for just the price of a telephone call. Generally, unless you are willing to spend some money, you will only be able to get a trial version of the program which will stop working after a short period of time (usually 30 days). If you want to carry on using it after that you'll have to pay for it – often at a substantial discount over the normal retail price. To get your hands on the best of the freebies, try searching Download.com (www.download.com) and Tucows (www.tucows.com).

Where can I find the best online shops?

As the number of internet traders has increased, so have the directories that promise to tell you where to find them. One of the most popular shopping directories is Shopsmart (www.shopsmart.com) but our personal favourite is 2020 Shops (www.2020shops.com) which provides friendly reviews of each of the stores and a useful rating system to help you get started. If you want to compare prices before you buy, you can shop around quickly and easily with the excellent Hoojit (www.hoojit.com) or Kelkoo (uk.kelkoo.com).

So many search engines, so little time – is there an alternative?

Funny you should ask! You can access the search engines listed above directly from The Zingin Search Guide (www.zingin.com/guide/search) and there's a complete listing of UK and global search tools in our Information Guide (www.zingin. com/guide/info/ search).

directories and department stores

Before you start shopping, you can find out what's available (and from where) with our guide to the best online directories and department stores.

Directories

The number of online shops is increasing at an incredible rate and it's almost impossible to keep track of who's selling what.

Unless you know exactly which shop you want to buy from (Harrods, for example), it's a good idea to check out your options on one of the larger shop directories before you start spending. Different directories offer different sets of features but the basic concept is the same: you type in what you want to buy and the directory gives you a list of traders that fit the bill. If you're buying on a budget, many of the directories will allow you to compare prices between hundreds of shops. You could argue that price comparison sites take the fun out of bargain hunting but at least you can be sure you're getting the best deal without spending hours browsing.

■ *The best of the best*

Kelkoo www.kelkoo.com

Another site that proves that the best internet companies are the ones with the silly names (Google? Yahoo!?). Kelkoo is a truly global shop comparison site and, although some countries are better represented than others, over 25,000 merchants from around the world are listed. If you've got plenty of time on your hands you can browse the entire directory yourself but it's much quicker to use the automated comparison system to sniff out the best price on books, music, films, games, computers, wine, electronics, toys, flights and a whole range of other stuff. Before you spend any money on the internet, make sure you shop around with this invaluable resource.

■ The rest of the best

2020 Shops www.2020shops.com

While Kelkoo is the online shopper's most powerful weapon, 2020 Shops is like a well-informed best mate. Other sites are busy developing automated shopping robots and search tools but this directory is trying to give internet shopping a friendly face. What really makes 2020 Shops stand out from the crowd is not their huge range of features (there's a definite lack of gimmicks) but rather the quality of the site reviews which have been written by professional journalists and are refreshingly honest and to the point. Whether you're buying a lamp or a lawnmower a quick visit to this excellent site will get you on the right track in no time.

Value Mad www.valuemad.co.uk

The internet does strange things to companies. ASDA stores may promote their old-fashioned values and cheap 'n' cheerful shopping experience but their Value Mad site is beyond funky. Split into three sections, the site allows you to get advice, find a shop and track down the latest hot deals, all with the aid of some colourful cartoon 'bots'. The number of retailers searched doesn't seem to be as thorough as Kelkoo and the information about each shop is certainly not up to the standard of 2020 Shops but if you are new to internet shopping and want that little bit of extra help, Value Mad should certainly be your first stop.

Shopsmart www.shopsmart.com

If you judge a shopping directory on the size of its popularity you'd find it hard to beat Shopsmart which is one of the busiest in the business. At the time of writing, there are over 2000 shops listed with more being added every day, making it one of the most complete sites of its type in the UK. As one of the first UK sites to offer price comparison technology, they've had plenty of time to get it right so it's a piece of cake to find the best deal on books, DVDs, games, music and video. The only downside to Shopsmart's popularity is that it lacks the friendliness that makes sites like 2020 Shops so usable but, if you're into cold hard facts, it's hard to criticise.

Y Bag www.ybag.com

Taking a different approach to price comparison, Y Bag makes the suppliers do the hard work so you don't have to. Once you've signed up for your free 'Y Bag' you simply type in details of what you want to buy ('I want to buy a fridge for under £500') and they'll send your request out to their network of suppliers via anonymous e-mail. If any of the suppliers think they have what you're looking for, they can send information directly to your Y Bag for you to pick up at your convenience. The great part is that because the system is completely anonymous, you won't get pestered by salesmen or junk mail – if a suitable quote arrives, you can get in touch with the seller but if not, there's no pressure. Well worth checking out if you're buying high-priced items. If you're looking for business products and services you'll find something similar at Mondus (www.mondus.co.uk).

Shops on the Net www.shopsonthenet.com

It may be just a directory of shops but this beautifully put together site contains enough online traders to make even the most hardened shopaholic admit defeat. Very similar in execution to 2020 Shops, the site rates each shop out of ten and also provides a mini review and some essential information to point you in the right direction. Some of the reviews are a little basic but, when you see how many shops are listed, you'll soon forgive them.

Buy www.buy.co.uk

Now this is a good idea. Buy's goal is to take the hassle out of finding the best deal on services like gas, electricity, water and mobile phones and it seems to be succeeding admirably.

After you've answered a few very straightforward questions, you'll be given a list of suggested packages and tariffs from all of the major suppliers. If you like what you see (and you probably will), you can simply click the 'buy' button to order online. Using the service is completely free and the advice is unbiased and very well informed. Nice.

■ *The best of the rest*

Hoojit www.hoojit.com

Hoojit may be the new kid on the shopping directory block but if its innovative approach to price comparison is anything to go by, it is destined to get very big, very quickly. Until then, you're probably still better off beginning your search at Kelkoo or 2020 Shops.

My Taxi www.mytaxi.co.uk

Offering you 'more time to have fun', My Taxi combines a shopping directory with a range of well-written articles and features. Having said that, considering how long they've been around, the service could be better. Worth a look.

No Bags www.nobags.com

No Bags is clearly going for the youth vote with this fresh and funky site. Everything's covered here from auctions to videos and the content is more than acceptable. The potential is here for something very impressive but at the moment it can't compete with the larger shopping directories.

Department stores and malls

Before we get into the nitty gritty of which is best, it might be a good idea to quickly explain the difference between an online department store and a mall. A department store on the web is pretty much identical to a department store on the high street – a big shop, owned by one company, which sells a wide range of products. Examples of these include Great Universal Stores (**www.greatuniversal.co.uk**) and Debenhams (**www.debenhams.co.uk**) which offer electrical goods, clothing, household items and much more, all from the one site.

An internet mall is a slightly different kettle of fish. Unlike department stores, internet malls basically bring together links to other people's shops (a bit like shopping directories), sometimes allowing you to pay for items from different merchants with just one order form. The original malls were created when internet shopping was in its infancy and people didn't know where to find the best shops. Nowadays they do seem a little out of place when you consider the popularity of directory sites but they are a great place to find specialist retailers who don't have a separate site of their own.

■ The best of the best

Great Universal www.greatuniversal.co.uk

The online arm of Great Universal Stores (GUS) doesn't fail to impress with this mammoth site. If you already have one of their paper catalogues you can use the online order form to speed things up or if you're a first-time visitor it's simple enough to browse through their incredible range of products. From nightwear to nit combs, boxer shorts to football kits, it's all here and with years of mail order experience you can expect great customer service and prompt delivery. Proof that traditional companies can make a killing on the web. *Huuuuge.*

■ The rest of the best

Shoppers Universe www.shoppersuniverse.com

Shoppers Universe may have been pipped at the post by GUS but it's certainly a close-run thing. Another massive range of products and plenty of those slightly bizarre things you always see in catalogues – Elysée 10 Pad Exercise System, anyone? The prices are extremely competitive and there's a handy gift finder so you can find the perfect microwave or set of spanners for the special person in your life.

Big Save www.bigsave.com

Imagine a huge department store which only exists on the web and so doesn't have to bump up prices to cover the cost of maintaining a high street shop. That's Big Save in a nutshell. Books, hi-fi equipment, clothing, toys, gadgets, computers... the list goes on and on and the prices are pretty competitive too. If you've got lots of shopping to do and not much time to do it – Big Save could well be the answer to your prayers.

Barclay Square www.barclaysquare.co.uk

As the name suggests, this mall is operated by Barclays Bank and features a range of specialist stores operated by some names you might not associate with retail. NME's CD store and the T3 Gadget Shop sit alongside Interflora and Choc Express to provide a balanced range of products all of which can be ordered without leaving the site. If you're concerned about the safety of online shopping, Barclays' involvement should give you the confidence to shop 'til you drop and as a member of the Which? Webtrader Scheme, you can expect a great level of service.

EshopOne www.eshopone.co.uk

Promising to offer quality products at internet prices, Eshop One is definitely catering for the higher end of the market with (amongst other things) handmade greetings cards, Derwent crystal and a range of British meats. Once you've filled your shopping basket and smashed through your spending limit, you can pay for all of the items at once in a secure shopping system which is backed up by the Which? Webtrader scheme.

Buckingham Gate www.buckinghamgate.co.uk

It feels expensive, it looks expensive and, you've guessed it, it is expensive. Buckingham Gate is the Harrods of online malls with merchants such as Rolls Royce, Clearwater Hampers, British Airways and Bentley. Not all of the shops require you to remortgage your house before you can start browsing though, with Interflora, Amivin and CD Classics offering lower-priced items in addition to their more expensive products. It's hard to fault the mall's design, and membership of Which? Web Trader and BT Trustwise should convince even the most nervous e-shopper to take the plunge.

■ The best of the rest

Argos www.argos.co.uk

Like many other high street retailers, Argos has decided not to offer its entire range online, concentrating instead on a selected range of special offers and products. If you have a copy of the Argos catalogue (who doesn't?) you can use the reference number to see if the product you want is available online and, if not, there's enough here to choose an alternative. Brighter shopping.

Debenhams www.debenhams.co.uk

After a shaky start, Debenhams is starting to make some serious waves on the web with their slick-looking site and trademark range of fashion, flowers and gifts. Ok, so there's nothing like the sort of range here that you'll find on the high street but if you don't mind sacrificing quantity for quality, you could do far worse.

Marks and Spencer www.marks-and-spencer.co.uk

From school wear to financial services, Marks and Spencer are quickly transferring their huge range of products and services onto the web. The layout is uncluttered and the photography, especially in the food section, is enough to make your mouth water. Superb.

QVC www.qvc.co.uk

The UK's favourite home shopping channel hits the web with a continually expanding range of electrical goods, fashion, home and garden essentials. The only problem QVC does have online is trying to whip up the excited frenzy used on TV to have impressionable shoppers reaching for the phone. Having said that, it's all very well designed and, if you're into gadgets, the site will have you tapping in your credit card number before you can say 'Wow that's amazing… how much does it cost? And it's not available in the shops? I'll take twenty.'

entertainment

If there's one thing that online shopping is good for, it's entertainment. Books, videos, DVDs, CDs and so much more can be bought at well below normal retail price and even hard-to-find titles are easy to track down. Entertainment superstores such as Amazon (**www.amazon.co.uk**) and Streets Online (**www.infront.co.uk**) claim to be able to satisfy all of your audio and visual needs but with new stores popping up every few days there are plenty of other options. If all this choice leaves you unsure where to start – worry no more – our run-down of the web's top retailers takes you straight to the best without wasting your time with the rest.

Entertainment superstores

If you don't fancy scouring the web for entertainment shops, there are plenty of retailers who can supply everything you need under one roof. Some of the superstores started selling one type of product (books in Amazon's case) but have since expanded into other markets while others (like WHSmiths) have always sold a wide range of items and continue to do so online.

The best of the best

Amazon www.amazon.co.uk

Predictable? Perhaps, but despite their comfortable market position, Amazon still continue to impress with their huge range and ultra-fast service. Books, videos, CVs and DVDs wrestle for shelf space and the prices for best-selling items are up to 50% off cover price. With the increasing popularity of price comparison sites many online entertainment stores are being forced to cut prices to the bone to remain competitive but when you've got everything you need in one place with service this good there's usually no need to go anywhere else.

■ *The rest of the best*

Streets Online www.infront.co.uk

In the UK only Streets Online come anywhere near Amazon in terms of customer service and range of products. Rather than being a 'we sell everything' superstore, Streets Online have set up individual shops to sell music, DVDs, games and books, all at extremely competitive prices and delivered in just a few days. In our experience, Amazon's delivery is that little bit quicker but, if you don't mind waiting, you'll find everything you need without breaking the bank. Visit Audiostreet (www.audiostreet.co.uk) for music, Gamestreet (www.gamesstreet.co.uk) for games, Alphabetstreet (www.alphabetstreet.co.uk) for books and DVDStreet (www.dvdstreet.co.uk) for … yup, you've guessed it.

Jungle www.jungle.com

It's a bit tricky to pigeon-hole Jungle as it manages to be half entertainment superstore and half computer retailer. Music, video, games and computer hardware are all available at extremely competitive prices and, after a few initial teething problems, customer service is now up there with the best. One of the few companies (along with Streets Online) who could threaten Amazon's market share.

WHSmith Online www.whsmith.co.uk

Unlike some of its competitors, the high street's favourite newsagent and bookshop is obviously taking this whole internet thing very seriously indeed. As you'd expect, there are plenty of books (over 1.5 million in fact!), including the latest best sellers and some old favourites, but there's also a wide range of chart CDs, magazines, stationery, software, films and all of the other stuff you'd find in your local branch. What might surprise you is how competitive the prices are, a few of which would make Amazon weep, and, if you're not in a buying mood, there's plenty to see and do on the site. Great prices, huge range, a trusted name. Enough said. For more magazines see Magazine Shop (www.magazineshop.co.uk).

Books

Bookworms rejoice! Selling books on the internet may seem a little strange considering that the web was supposed to spell the end for traditional publishing but booksellers are making a killing online. The original was Amazon (see Entertainment superstores) but competition is heating up and there are some excellent bargains to be found if you know where to look – which is where we come in…

■ *The best of the best*

Book Brain **www.bookbrain.co.uk**
Bookbrain is one of those sites that makes the internet worth using. The site doesn't actually sell any books itself, acting instead as a price comparison service for the big names in the business. Basically, you type in the name of the book you want and it will scour the most popular UK booksellers for the best price. It's very straightforward and you can usually make a decent saving from the normal cover price – what more could you ask for? For more of the same see Directories in Chapter 2.

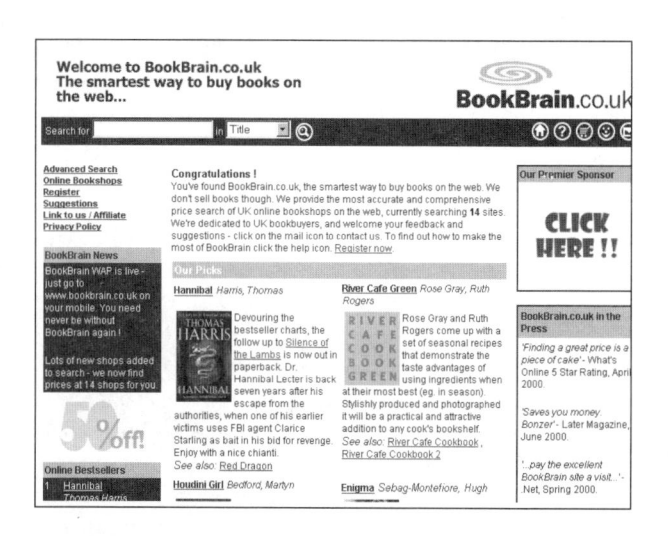

■ The rest of the best

BOL www.uk.bol.com

Judging a bookseller by the size of its range is a bit redundant these days as everyone seems to sell every book. You can't, however, fail to be impressed with a site offering over 1.5 million books at around 30% off cover price. In addition to the shop itself, there are interviews with famous authors, plenty of gift ideas and some of the best book descriptions you'll find. Add in BOL's regular (and impressive) special offers and you have the recipe for retail heaven.

Waterstones Online www.waterstones.co.uk

An impressive offering from the high street favourite. Waterstones Online features the usual (huge) range of books and is also one of the first UK booksellers to offer downloadable electronic books. If you order through the site, you'll have to pay a small extra charge for postage but you can get around that by having your order delivered to your nearest store. There's nothing particularly special about the design or layout of the site – although it looks very nice – but if you want to buy a book, it's as simple as can be.

Alphabet Street www.alphabetstreet.co.uk
Part of the Streets Online empire, Alphabet Street stocks a huge range of books at great prices. A firm favourite.

Online Originals www.onlineoriginals.com
Proving that not all bookshops are the same, Online Originals specialises in downloadable electronic versions of work from new authors. Fiction, non-fiction, drama and youth are all well represented and the quality of writing is comparable with more traditional books. Having said that, if you're looking for a cheap alternative to buying pieces of dead tree then you'll need to look elsewhere – each download costs about £4 and unless you have a handheld PC or plenty of printer paper you won't be able to read the books on the train. Except for the satisfaction of helping struggling new authors, there's no real advantage to downloadable books but the quality of the work makes it worth taking a look.

■ *The best of the rest*

Basically Books www.basicallybooks.co.uk
Buying books for the under-13s just got a whole lot easier. Basically Books specialise in children's titles and their

straightforward-to-browse site offers helpful plot summaries and a guide to which age groups each title is best suited.

Booklovers www.booklovers.co.uk

Booklovers specialise in tracking down second-hand and out-of-print books. The site is based around a very simple-to-use search system and if you can't find the title you're looking for, Booklovers will try their hardest to get it for you. Superb prices and the site works like a dream. If you have no luck try the Amazon-owned American alternative, Bibliofind (www.bibliofind.com).

Music

If music be the food of love, you can get very fat indeed on the web. Like books, music is extremely popular in the world of e-commerce as it doesn't cost much to post and fits easily through your letterbox. It's certainly a melting pot, with music from multi-platinum artists sharing cyber-shelf space with new talent and, despite piracy fears, many artists are starting to allow you to download tracks direct to your computer.

■ *The best of the best*

Audiostreet www.audiostreet.co.uk

Streets Online do it again with this extremely well-stocked site. The UK top 40 are all present and correct and it's not too shoddy on the old stuff either. One of the first UK stores to offer music DVDs. See page 29 for web picture.

■ *The rest of the best*

101 CD www.101cd.com

Although 101 CD is a definite contender for the top spot, the fact that Streets Online is just that little bit slicker allows it to claim the title. Operated from a real-life high-street music shop, 101 offers a truly massive range of CDs to suit every conceivable musical taste. The real selling point here, though, is that 101 are able to get hold of hard-to-find albums by importing them from Europe and America. Yes, you wait a bit longer for some of the more obscure titles but when you've already spent weeks looking for something, it's a price worth paying. If you want top 40 tunes then

Audiostreet probably have the upper hand but if you want to relive your musical youth, there's only one place to come.

MP3.com www.mp3.com

In case the name hasn't given it away, MP3.com allows you to download music from new artists (and a few established ones) either free of charge or for a small fee. Unlike the thousands of illegal MP3 sites on the web, this one is totally legit so you can download tracks without looking over your shoulder for the copyright police. It looks great, the tracks download quickly and the tunes aren't bad either. To download some of the best MP3 software in the business, visit Music Match (**www.musicmatch.com**) or Sonique (**www.sonique.com**).

PeopleSound www.peoplesound.com

The British answer to MP3.com has some excellent talent on show and because it's UK based you won't have to endure an endless stream of American teen garage bands. There's plenty of free music available and if you find an artist you like, you can find out more about them and even buy their CD. Become a talent scout without leaving your computer. Rock and Roll.

Boxman www.boxman.co.uk

Boxman started life as a CD retailer – and a very good one too. Like so many others, though, it has clearly decided that there's money to be made from films and games and so has become an entertainment superstore. The prices are certainly competitive and the site tries very hard to be hip but if you're looking for anything except music, you'll probably find more elsewhere.

Borrow Or Rob www.borroworrob.com

By taking up more than its fair share of Rs and Os Borrow Or Rob clearly wants to make it as hard as possible to type its web address. If you do manage to get everything in the right order though, you'll find a pretty nice music site offering some unbeatable prices on the latest albums, some of which can be had for under £9.

Vitiminic www.vitiminic.co.uk

Despite sounding like an online chemist, Vitiminic is actually one of the most popular downloadable music sites in the UK. It's easy enough to browse and there's a nice mix of genres to keep everyone happy. Smart.

■ *The best of the rest*

CD Wow www.cdwow.co.uk

Don dark glasses and try not to look directly at the screen when you visit CD Wow. The prices are certainly low (although not always as cheap as Borrow or Rob) and there's a decent range available but someone needs to have a word about the use of the colour yellow. Blinding.

Replay www.replay.co.uk

If you're a DJ (or older than fourteen) this could be your idea of heaven. Specialising in rare vinyl, Replay has a great range of dance, jazz, rock and reggae albums and a few singles thrown in for good measure. Dig deep enough and you'll find some true classics. If you're still looking try Hard to Find (www.hard-to-find.co.uk) or for more dancey stuff, check out Ministry of Sound (www.ministryofsound.co.uk).

Tower Europe www.towereurope.com
The digital arm of Tower Records is well worth a browse for regular visitors to their real-world stores. Nothing special but nothing to criticise.

Icrunch www.icrunch.com
Another UK MP3 site, this time with a greater emphasis on features and news as well as the downloads themselves. The site looks great and the features are well written but it does lack some of the range of MP3.com and PeopleSound.

Video and DVD

From *Mission Impossible* to *My Left Foot*, no matter what your cinematic preferences, you'll find something suitable on the web. Although DVD is fast taking over from video as the format of choice for new releases, there's still plenty to choose from on both formats – all at suitably internety prices. Ordering the best of the silver screen from the comfort of your computer screen couldn't be easier.

■ *The best of the best*

Blackstar www.blackstar.co.uk
If you've ever ordered from Blackstar you'll know that there could be no competition for the best of the best video and DVD retailer. Their stock is truly huge but that's not all – excellent service, excellent prices, intelligent reviews, clear yet stylish design and prompt delivery make Blackstar one of the web's true retail success stories. See page 33 for web picture.

■ The rest of the best

Filmworld www.filmworld.co.uk

Making an informed purchase couldn't be simpler at Filmworld which provides extremely detailed background information about every film it stocks. Browsing is simple enough but if you want to go directly to your favourite, you can search by title, director, lead actor or year of release. It's even possible to try before you buy with a nice selection of online trailers. Nice.

DVD Street www.dvdstreet.co.uk

The Streets folk earn another place in our hearts with this film-buff-friendly site. Searchable stock listings, short but sweet reviews and keen pricing make this a great place to look for both new releases and re-mastered classics. As the name suggests, the emphasis is on shiny disks rather than magnetic tape but then video is *soooo* last century.

Blockbuster www.blockbuster.co.uk

On the high street Blockbuster may be the video rental champions but on the web they're more interested in selling you the latest releases. Both videos and DVDs are available and if you still want to rent, there's a list of your nearest stores.

MovieTrak www.movietrak.com

If you can't justify buying a DVD then Movietrak are more than happy to let you rent them online. Simply choose from their well-stocked range of titles and they'll send you your DVD for seven days. Once you've finished with it, simply chuck it into the pre-paid envelope provided and send it back. It's a simple enough idea and it doesn't cost much more than renting from your local video shop. Sorry Blockbuster, but someone beat you to it.

■ *The best of the rest*

BBC Shop www.bbcshop.com

As you browse through the range of drama, comedy, documentary and educational programming here you suddenly realise how much excellent stuff the BBC is responsible for. From *This Life* to *The Tellytubbies* you'll find something for all the family. Put us down for a Wallace and Grommit box set.

DVD World www.dvdworld.co.uk

The name is a bit of a giveaway. DVD players are available in addition to the shiny little fellas themselves and there's plenty of background information for fans of the fast-growing format.

Film Store www.filmstore.co.uk
When a company like Odeon build a film site you expect something pretty special – and Filmstore doesn't disappoint. The design may be a little too dark and moody for some but you can't fault their choice of titles which include some true cult classics as well as the latest blockbusters. If you prefer to watch films on the big screen make sure you also check out Odeon's excellent ticket booking system (www.odeon.co.uk).

Looking for something to play your new DVDs and Videos on? See Chapter 4 Computers and technology.

Games

We're not talking Monopoly here. If computer or console games are your thing then you'll be spoilt for choice online. To avoid confusion, we've only listed suppliers who *specialise* in games here. There are plenty of sites which offer games along with other types of PC software but rather than mixing them in with the games, you'll find companies such as PC World (www.pcworld.co.uk) in Chapter 4 Computers and technology.

■ *The best of the best*

UR Wired www.urwired.com
Definitely one for the dedicated gamer, UR Wired looks stunning and doesn't disappoint on the price front either. Their feature-packed online magazine makes keeping up to

date with the latest game news and reviews easy and with dedicated sections for each format, you'll only get the information that you really want. Before you buy any games, make sure you compare prices between Games Street and UR Wired – they're both gaming heaven.

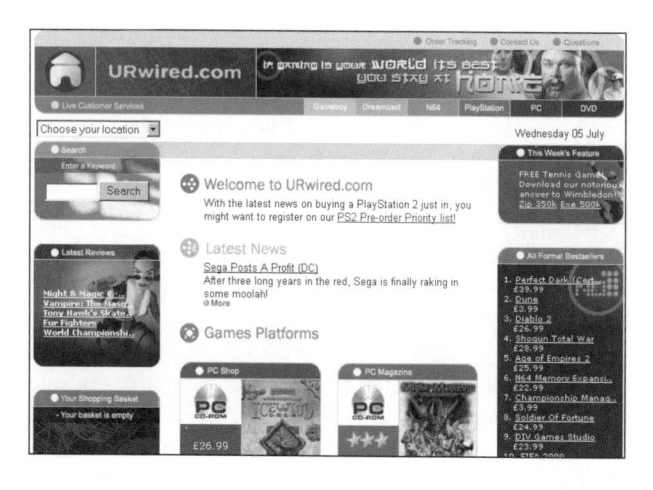

■ The rest of the best

Games Street www.gamesstreet.co.uk

While UR Wired is clearly trying to be a magazine as well as a shop, Game Street is happy just being a great source of the latest titles at extremely competitive prices. If you're new to internet shopping, you can buy here with confidence, knowing that they are one of the UK's largest online traders. Ok, if you are looking for up-to-the-minute game news, cheats and big pictures of Lara Croft you'll probably want to try somewhere else but if you just want to buy games – it's hard to fault.

Special Reserve www.reserve.co.uk

A definite contender for our 'how much information can you fit on the page at one time' award, Special Reserve have developed a site which is literally packed full of games, hardware, reviews, cheats and other gamey stuff. For less than £7 a year you can join the Special Reserve club which will save you money on their already discounted prices. Special.

Gameplay www.gameplay.com

Gameplay has been around in different forms for ages but has recently morphed into something truly unique. Naturally, if you want to buy games, you'll find a very well-stocked shop but there is so much more to discover. Online gamers will love Wireplay, a free service allowing you to compete against other players across the 'net, and the bizarrely titled *Spank!* magazine which is capable of mixing it with the best of them. Gameplay looks absolutely stunning and, unlike many Flash-enabled sites, it loads extremely quickly – probably the sexiest game site on the web.

■ *The best of the rest*

Games Paradise www.gamesparadise.com

Games Paradise is part of the WHSmith Online group but still manages to retain some of its own individuality. The prices and range of products are no more outstanding than other games sites but the fact that it's supported by such a huge high street name makes it a safe bet for first-time buyers.

4

computers and technology

It makes a whole lot of sense to sell computers and electrical equipment on the web given the number of technology enthusiasts who use it. As you'd expect, there are loads of sites offering computer hardware and software but there are also a growing number of companies selling TVs, fridges, hi-fis, phones, kettles and even toasters online. If you're a gadget fan, you'll also want to check out some of the more quirky items in Chapter 12 Toys and gifts.

Computer hardware

Computer retailers and manufacturers were quick to realise the potential of selling their wares on the internet. From floppy disks through to entire systems, it's all here – often at prices that laugh in the face of the high street stores. If you are spending serious money on a computer system you need to be confident that you'll get help if something goes wrong. Before you decide to part with your hard-earned cash it's important to check the site's returns and support policy and, as a general rule, if they don't provide a customer service phone number – walk away.

■ The best of the best

PC World www.pcworld.co.uk

Not satisfied with owning huge chunks of retail space around the country, PC World have started their domination of the web with this surprisingly well-put-together site. Software, hardware, downloads and even furniture are available at (usually) the same price as you'll find them on the high street and the site's search system makes it easy to find what you're looking for. Bargain hunters will want to look elsewhere for massive savings but if you're more concerned about getting top brand equipment at reasonable prices, PC World is definitely a name you can trust.

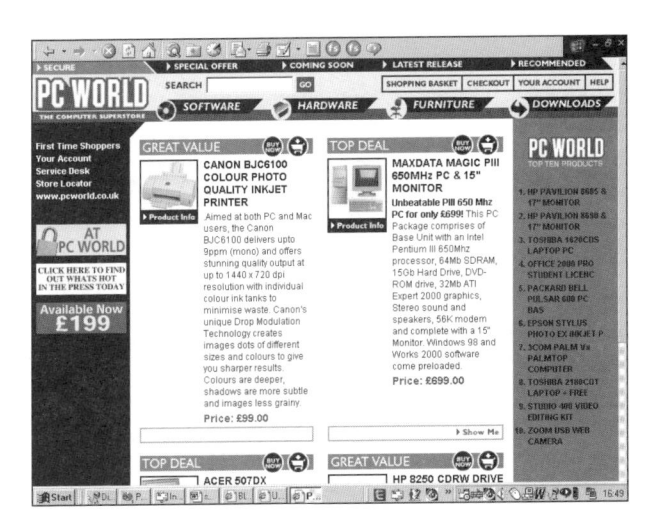

■ *The rest of the best*

Micro Warehouse www.microwarehouse.co.uk

Computers, printers, software, mice and even some Mac stuff – every page of the Micro Warehouse site is packed with the latest technology at some pretty reasonable prices. Like PC World, the company has been around for years so you should be able to trust them to look after you and, as they are part of the BT Trustwise scheme, your money is safe too.

Apple www.apple.com/uk

If you're a Mac fan then you can cut out the middleman altogether with this superb effort from the comeback kids. Like everything that Apple have produced in the past few years, the site has that funky transparent colourful plasticy feel and is certainly the coolest computer site on the web (think Gap meets PC World). If the glossy pictures and hip young models give you the urge to actually buy something then you won't be disappointed – Apple's shop is one of the best too, with fast delivery and the confidence that comes with buying direct from the manufacturer. Even if you're a die-hard PC user, you'll be tempted.

Dell www.dell.co.uk

Another company famed for selling their own products directly. Dell allows you to create your dream machine with as many (or as few) extras as you want. The prices are certainly not cheap but their quality is almost legendary. Each machine is custom built (naturally) so expect a short wait before your new computer arrives.

Evesham www.evesham.com

Evesham have years of experience in the PC mail order business and certainly know what their customers want. Behind the site's flashy front-end lies an extremely user-friendly order system which allows you to build a PC to your own specifications. If you're looking for big brands like Packard Bell and Sony then you'll need to look elsewhere but Evesham's own-brand products are reliable and affordable so does the badge on the front really matter?

Gateway www.gw2k.co.uk

Once famous for using cows in their advertising, you can still see evidence of Gateway's bovine obsession dotted around their site. Cows aside, as the company only sell directly rather than through retailers, it's very straightforward to place an order (it has to be). Simply choose a system, decide on the specifications you need, and proceed to the checkout… and that's no bull.

Elonex www.elonex.co.uk

Although Elonex supply plenty of kit to schools, businesses and the England Rugby Team (according to the site), they still have plenty to offer the home user. Like Dell, Evesham and the rest, you can customise your PC by adding or taking away until you're happy with everything – a bit like very expensive Lego.

Software Paradise www.softwareparadise.co.uk

Software Paradise have been around since 1986 and judging by the customer testimonials on this busy site – they certainly know what they're doing. No matter whether you're a beginner, a business user, a developer or a fully fledged geek, there's something for you here and if years of experience and plenty of happy customers aren't enough to convince you to buy then look for the Which? Web Trader logo and the ISO9002 accreditation. Very nice.

■ The best of the rest

Dabs www.dabs.com
Don't let the cluttered design put you off. There are some excellent bargains to be had if you dig deep enough.

Maplin www.maplin.co.uk
If you fancy getting your hands a bit dirty by building your own PC then a visit to Maplin is a must. From processors to power supplies via monitors and screwdrivers – it's all here at prices that won't cause any headaches.

Mesh www.meshplc.co.uk
Guess what? Yes, you've guessed it, Mesh allow you to customise your PC to fit your exact requirements. Once you've recovered from that earth-shattering innovation there is a more than adequate range of computer hardware and software to browse through.

Simply www.simply.co.uk
Still not tired of companies who let you customise your PC? Good news for Simply…

Viglen www.viglen.co.uk
… and Viglen.

Electrical superstores

Buying a book on the internet is one thing… but a fridge? It may take some getting used to but there are some huge savings to be made by buying online. Although the big high street names such as Dixons (www.dixons.co.uk) are happy to take your money, you'll find some of the best deals from independent retailers like Unbeatable (www.unbeatable.co.uk). As with any expensive online purchase, it's very important to check out the supplier before you hand over your credit card number. You shouldn't have any problems from any of our recommended companies but it's still a good idea to check the site's returns policy and after-sales support before you sign on the line.

■ *The best of the best*

Comet www.comet.co.uk

This site from the high street favourite seems to have it all – a trusted name, competitive prices, a huge range (over 2000 products) and an extremely professional-looking site. If you're bargain hunting, you will definitely want to shop around as you will find better elsewhere and Comet only guarantee to match prices found in other high street shops and not on the web. Having said that, if you would rather pay a few pounds extra to have that extra peace of mind – you know where to come. See page 44 for web picture.

■ *The rest of the best*

Unbeatable www.unbeatable.co.uk

They're not wrong, you know. Unbeatable's prices are

generally much lower than you'll see elsewhere and there's a huge range of electrical equipment to choose from so you won't have any problems finding what you're looking for. The appearance of the site leaves a little to be desired, but at least you're not paying extra to cover the cost of expensive web designers and the presence of the Which? Web Trader logo means you can be confident that your order will arrive promptly and safely. Proof that you can't judge a book by its cover.

Quality Electrical Direct www.qed-uk.com

If you don't find the product you want at Unbeatable then it's well worth trying this equally frills-free alternative. Claiming to offer the UK's largest range of electrical and gas appliances, the site certainly does have a massive range of TVs, videos, hi-fis, camcorders, cameras, fridges, freezers, cookers, washers, dryers and just about anything else you could possibly want. The really nice thing about QED is their SMS quote feature which allows you to instantly check the price of an electrical item using any text message enabled mobile. Next time you're standing in Dixons – why not make the sales assistant's day by instantly comparing QED's prices? Hours of fun.

21 Store www.21store.com

21 Store claims to 'know digital' and their site proves that they know how to sell it too. Specialising in digital equipment and gadgets, they have a good range of palmtops, mobile phones and GPS systems and certainly know what they're talking about when it comes to describing the products. If you're into gadgets (or a James Bond fan) this could well be your idea of heaven.

Easy Buy www.easibuy.com

There's audio, video, garden equipment, kitchenware, cameras, vacuum cleaners, phones and so much more on this well-stocked but understated site. The prices on offer are usually considerably below high street prices and a slick ordering system makes buying from the site, er, easy.

Dixons www.dixons.co.uk

Considering that Dixons have changed the face of the internet with Freeserve you'd expect something pretty innovative from their electrical retail arm. Unfortunately, while there's nothing wrong with this site, there's certainly nothing outstanding either. All of the usual range of products are present and correct and the prices compare favourably with other high street retailers – it does the job but doesn't really impress.

■ *The best of the rest*

Battery Factory **www.batteryfactory.co.uk**
This electrical stuff is all well and good but without batteries you won't get very far. For massive savings on power in all shapes and sizes this is the site for you.

Hi-fi

Most of the major electrical retailers will be able to provide all of the hi-fi equipment you need for a decent home set-up or to keep listening on the move but if you want something a bit special, you'll want to head for one of the many specialist suppliers who are setting up on the web.

■ *The best of the best*

Richer Sounds **www.richersounds.co.uk**
Richer regulars will be please to find that the Richer Sounds' site is every bit as 'in your face' as their chain of shops. A recent redesign has created a very pleasant shopping experience with plenty of photos of the equipment and some superb prices. Anyone suffering from e-shopping safety paranoia will love the security measures in place here – not only is the order system located on a secure server but the server itself is housed in an ex-MOD underground bunker. We kid you not.

■ The rest of the best

Hi-Fi Bitz www.hifibitz.co.uk

Hi-fi and home cinema separates are the name of the game here with a very broad selection of brand name products. The shopping system is not the most high tech in the business but it's simple enough to use and as everything is backed up by the Which? Web Trader logo, you can buy with confidence.

Purley Radio www.purleyradio.co.uk

Video may have killed the radio star but the radios themselves are alive and kicking on the web thanks to great sites like this. No matter what type of wireless you're after, you'll find something to fit the bill at Purley's, including the famous Trevor Baylis clockwork model as well as top brands like Sony, Grundig, Roberts and Bush. Don't worry about hidden delivery charges – all prices include 48-hour delivery so the price you see is the price you pay.

Techtronics www.techtronics.com

The design of this site may be a little unconventional but the products available are nothing less than cutting edge. There are MP3 players, DVD, smart cards and some nifty home cinema stuff and impatient shoppers will be pleased to hear that you can track your order online.

Blue Spot www.bluespot.co.uk

In-car entertainment is not very well represented on the web but if you don't mind restricting yourself to one brand (Blaupunkt) then Blue Spot is an excellent place to start. There are photographs of the entire range with an easy-to-use ordering system if you're tempted to spend some money – and with savings of up to 30% on some models, that's a very definite possibility.

Mobile phones

To say that mobile phones are popular is like calling Michael Jackson 'a bit eccentric'. In the past few years portable telephony has exploded and, to the annoyance of train passengers everywhere, almost everyone has got one. The recent emergence of mobile internet (WAP) has given the market another huge shot in the arm by giving everyone another reason to upgrade to a new handset. All of the network operators are selling direct to customers on the internet and a growing number of independent retailers have sprung up to capitalise on customers' confusion over tariffs and phones. Don't automatically assume that by buying direct from the operator you'll save any money – many of them stick rigidly to the normal retail price – whereas companies like Carphone Warehouse (**www.carphonewarehouse.co.uk**)

run regular promotions and sales. If you want to buy directly from the network operators but need some impartial advice, it's also worth checking out Buy (www.buy.co.uk). So, you want to buy a phone but don't know where to go first? Read on…

■ *The best of the best*

The Carphone Warehouse www.carphonewarehouse.co.uk

No matter where you live, you'll probably be only a few miles from your nearest Carphone Warehouse store. Not satisfied with owning hundreds of shops around the country, the company has built an excellent site to encourage customers to buy online. One of the major benefits of buying from the Carphone Warehouse is their friendly, impartial advice and they've obviously made a big effort to carry this over onto the site. Simply answer a few questions about your budget, how often you plan to use the phone etc. and the site will suggest the right handset and tariff for you. If you like what they suggest (and you almost certainly will) then it only takes a couple of clicks to place your order. It looks great and works perfectly.

■ *The rest of the best*

Miah Telecom **www.miah-telecom.co.uk**
They may not have such a recognisable brand name but in terms of range and prices, they are more than capable of competing with the best of them. If you're not sure what type of phone is right for you, you'll find plenty of helpful advice to point you in the right direction, and once you've picked your handset and tariff the prices are extremely competitive. When you come to buy your next phone simply compare prices between Carphone Warehouse and Miah and see which works out best for you – you can expect the same range of service from both of them.

Phone Factory **www.phonefactory.com**
Aimed squarely at the younger consumer, Phone Factory is a fun and friendly way to buy pay-as-you-go mobiles. Beattie and her team of cute cartoon character chums act as guides to the site and are always happy to offer advice – even if you don't need it – and when you've finished shopping there's a screensaver to download and an utterly pointless but strangely addictive card game thing to play. The phones themselves are not overpriced but there's no huge discounts either – bargain hunters will find better elsewhere, but the site looks great and will certainly appeal to its target audience. Slick, cheerful, cute and painless.

Beyond 2000 **www.beyond-2000.co.uk**
You might think that a site billing itself as 'The World's premier mobile phone boutique' is just asking for trouble but, in Beyond 2000's case, it could certainly put up a good fight. There are no phones available here, just a massive

array of accessories for just about any handset on the market and the prices are among the best we've found. If you need a replacement aerial, an in-car charger or a cool leather case, you'll find it all here.

■ The best of the rest

Although you'll rarely get the best deal by going directly to the mobile operator, if you do want the peace of mind of dealing direct you'll definitely want to check out the following official sites.

BT Cellnet www.btcellnet.co.uk

Trying so very hard to be hip, BT Cellnet have developed an uncluttered if slightly confusing web presence which allows you to browse their range and, of course, buy online. The prices are far from spectacular so unless you own shares in Cellnet, you'll probably be better off looking at an independent retailer.

Orange www.orange.co.uk

Like BT Cellnet, Orange have decided to go for the 'we're so cool it hurts' angle but so far haven't quite managed to pull it off. The site looks nice enough but when it comes to actually spending money, it's a bit of a chore.

Vodafone www.vodafone-retail.co.uk

Definitely one of the more impressive official sites. Once you've chosen your handset and tariff from the Vodafone range and provided your credit card information via their secure server, you can expect delivery of your new phone in 24 hours.

clothing and fashion

Although the number of online clothing retailers continues to grow, the simple fact is that clothes are one of the hardest things to buy over the web. No matter how hard they try, internet traders cannot allow you to try on a pair of shoes or a shirt before you buy. What they can (and usually do) offer, however, is a decent returns policy so that if the cap doesn't fit – you don't have to wear it. Before buying it's important to find out what you can do if you buy the wrong size, colour or style and, more importantly, how much you'll be charged for returning items. To be fair, most clothing e-tailers will offer a free, no-quibble returns policy but there are still a few who will refuse to refund or replace purchases. This is especially true of swimwear and shoes so make sure you ask before you buy. For more clothing don't forget to check out Department stores and malls in Chapter 2.

Clothing stores

Clothes shopaholics will be pleased to find some of the high street's biggest names on the web. From Topshop and Topman to Kays and Evans they've all got in on the act and if you want the best brands at the lowest prices, some of the internet-only companies are well worth checking out. For sportswear see Chapter 7 Sports and outdoor.

■ The best of the best

Zoom www.zoom.co.uk

More than just a clothing store, this joint effort from the Arcadia Group stores (Topshop, Dorothy Perkins et al.) provides a wealth of lifestyle features as well as some pretty impressive online clothes shopping. The fact that the site is operated by such a recognisable name allows you to order with confidence, knowing that if it doesn't fit you shouldn't have too many problems getting things sorted. We like.

■ The rest of the best

Kays www.kaysnet.com

Catalogue shoppers – this one's for you. The Kays catalogue is famous for providing stylish clothing at very reasonable prices and their online version is no different. You can search by catalogue number or simply browse their easy-to-use online shop to choose your new wardrobe. Kays have years of experience in mail order so once you've filled your shopping basket you can be confident that your clothes will arrive quickly and safely. Very nice.

Haburi www.haburi.com
In a nutshell, Haburi offers branded clothing at factory outlet prices. The site excels in its range of casual wear with most of the world's top brands making an appearance, sometimes at less than half the usual price. The layout of the site is uncluttered yet impressive and ordering is straightforward enough – great if you want to be seen in designer clothes without paying designer prices.

Dressmart www.dressmart.co.uk
Belts, bags, T-shirts, trousers, shirts, socks and all things trendy are to be found on this slick-looking site. The products are well presented with some clear photographs to show you exactly what you're buying before you part with your money and there are plenty of brand names to keep even the most hardened fashion victim happy.

Topman www.topman.co.uk
Like Zoom, Topman is trying very hard to be seen as a lifestyle magazine as well as a place to buy clothes. Music, dating, jokes and plenty of pictures of 'cooler than thou' models complement the online shopping system to make this a must-visit site for trendy folk.

Swerve www.swerve.co.uk

The design may not inspire you to whip out your credit card but the prices probably will. Armani, Versace, Calvin Klein, D&G, Valentino, Diesel, Ralph Lauren, Timberland, Tommy Hilfiger, Yves Saint Laurent, Thomas Burberry, DKNY and the rest are all discounted and Swerve even promise to beat any price found on another UK website. The site displays the Which? Web Trader logo, meaning that ordering should be suitably painless.

Into Fashion www.intofashion.com

If you're the type of person who always looks at the label first, Into Fashion could well be the site for you. The impressive-looking shop is full of T-shirts 'as worn by Zoe Ball' and trousers 'loved by Kate Moss' but behind all the name dropping there is actually a very user-friendly ordering system. The clothes looks great and the site works exactly as it should – but cheap it ain't.

■ *The best of the rest*

AW Rust www.awrust.co.uk

AW Rust exist both online and in the real world with a shop in Essex and one of the UK's best-looking clothing retail sites. The company specialise in leatherwear from brands like Urban Stone, Gas, French Connection and more.

Best of British www.thebestofbritish.com

Show a little national pride with clothing (and more) from some of Britain's top designers, including Frost French, Janet Reger and Toby Mott. Cool Britannia.

Bumps Maternity www.bumpsmaternity.com
Pregnant? Check out this fresh and funky site offering a nice range of maternity wear.

Evans www.evans.ltd.uk
Another winner from the Arcadia group. Impressive range and an easy-to-use ordering system.

Novelty Togs www.noveltytogs.com
The best place to get hold of those South Park socks and Homer Simpson boxer shorts you've always wanted.

Top brands

Rather than dragging your mouse around huge clothing superstores, the internet makes it easier than ever to buy directly from some of fashion's biggest names and to discover new brands from the UK and across the globe. Although most labels have some sort of web presence, only a relatively small number are using the 'net as one of their main channels of distribution so don't expect a huge amount of choice. We've only listed sites which allow UK customers to order online but if you just want to find your nearest store then it's worth doing a quick search on your favourite search engine for sites like the impressive Paul Smith (www.paulsmith.co.uk) which contains plenty of product info but, at the time of writing, no shopping facility.

■ *The best of the best*

Fat Face www.fatface.co.uk
They may not be the UK's best known brand but when it comes to the web, Fat Face are definitely at the top of the

tree. The emphasis of the range is on comfort and there's something for everyone – whether you're a sports enthusiast or just want something to chill out in, and the kids' range (Brat Face) should suit even the most fashion-conscious youngster. Clear photography ensures that you know exactly what you're buying and the ordering process couldn't be simpler. A British site that's one of the best in the world.

■ The rest of the best

Diesel www.diesel.co.uk

Diesel's virtual store contains everything you'd find in one of their normal real-world shops even down to the (virtual) changing room and (virtual) shop assistant. The clothes aren't bad either with menswear, ladies' wear, denim, fragrances and even luggage – all obtainable at the click of a mouse. Diesel have clearly put some serious effort (and money) into transferring their brand online and, unlike many of their fellow labels, they've done an excellent job. The navigation system may a little quirky but it does the job and you'll soon get used to it.

Skim www.skim.com

Who? Skim may not be the biggest name in fashion just yet but we think they're destined for great things. Each item in the range comes with its very own unique Skim number plastered across the front, the idea being that if you see someone interesting wearing one, you can visit Skim.com and send them a message. Ok, it's a bit of a bizarre idea and the clothes seem to be designed for very skinny people but it's already huge in Zurich and, because you can order online, it won't be long before you start seeing Skim numbers on a street near you.

La Redoute www.redoute.co.uk

Continental style from the internet's fashion capital. The site itself is extremely well put together with separate sections for men, women, sportswear and children's fashion. Very cool, very stylish and very, very French.

Shoes and accessories

So, you've picked your perfect outfit and typed in your credit card number – now it's just a question of waiting for your order to arrive. In the meantime why not complete the look with some stylish accessories? Shoes, lingerie, socks and even watches – accessorising has never been so much fun.

■ The best of the best

Shoe Shop www.shoe-shop.com

Europe's largest online shoe shop offers thousands of styles – all delivered free to anywhere in the UK. The site used to be let down by some very cluttered design but a recent makeover has left behind an extremely flash-looking shop with a user-friendly ordering system that makes spending money a pleasure. The prices on offer are already excellent but if you do see anything cheaper elsewhere, make sure you let Shoe Shop know and they'll refund the difference. In the unlikely event that Shoe Shop doesn't satisfy your footwear requirements, check out Shoe World (www.shoeworld.com) for links to a whole world of alternatives.

■ *The rest of the best*

Accessorize www.accessorize.co.uk

If bright nail polishes, novelty hair clips and sarongs are your kind of thing, you'll be in accessory heaven when you visit Accessorize. There's a very 'More Magazine' feel about the site's design which centres on photos of models who are clearly far too old to be wearing medium stripe flip-flops and lots of advice on 'how to make the first move on the boy you fancy'. Having said that, they clearly know their target audience and the shopping system is extremely easy to use, with nice touches like the e-boyfriend who promises to keep you up to date on all Accessorize special offers and promotions. If you love the shop, you'll love the site but it's definitely one for the girlies.

Easy Shop www.easyshop.co.uk

Claiming to be 'virtually the greatest underwear store in the world', Easy Shop certainly is up there with the best. Both men and women are catered for, with leading brands such as Brassmonkey and Wonderbra and more than sixty others. When it comes to spending money, the shop certainly lives up to its name with an extremely straightforward shopping system, no-quibble returns and free delivery. The real winner here though is the well-thought-out range of extra services available to internet shoppers. If you need a bit of help choosing the right garment you'll love the bras, briefs and legs finder while secret romantics (and stalkers) will make good use of the Easy Shop virtually anonymous option. As if excellent features, a flawless ordering system and a huge range weren't enough, there's even the all-important Which? Web Trader logo to provide extra peace of mind. Spot on.

Marcus Shoes www.marcusshoes.com

Sam Marcus has been delivering Loake shoes to London's office workers since 1975 and with a client list which includes names such as ICI, the Bank of England, Rolls-Royce and Lloyd's of London you can be pretty sure that the quality is top notch. If you work in the City or Docklands, Sam will visit your office for a no-obligation fitting but if you live further afield, the mail order service means you won't have to miss out. Fast, friendly and definitely one of a kind.

■ The best of the rest

Ann Summers www.annsummers.co.uk

Lingerie and so much more – designed for more daring tastes. Not one for the kiddies. For more of the same but with a higher price tag, check out Agent Provocateur (www.agentprovocateur.com).

Brief Look www.brieflook.co.uk

Another site in the Easy Shop mould, Brief Look promises to take care of all of your lingerie requirements. Nice range and it looks good too.

Cruelty Free Shop www.crueltyfreeshop.com

Animal friendly, ethical, vegan products delivered to your door, straight from the supplier. If you love animals, you'll love this.

Smart Bras www.smartbras.com

As the name suggests, this site is home to some of the UK's leading bra brands. Looks good and ordering is simple. Enough said.

health and beauty

If you think about it, health and beauty products are extremely well suited to buying online as they usually come in small boxes, bottles and tubes which fit easily through your letterbox and (with the possible exception of make-up) you don't need to test them out before you buy. No matter if you're feeling under the weather or just want to keep young and beautiful, all of the lotions, potions and remedies your body needs are just a click away.

Health and beauty superstores

Online health and beauty stores are extremely popular on the other side of the Atlantic and are slowly starting to appear in the UK. High street favourites like Boots (**www.boots.co.uk**) are amongst the best in the business but there are plenty of other companies like All Cures (**www.all-cures.com**) who are giving them a serious run for their money so it's well worth shopping around.

■ The best of the best

All Cures www.allcures.com

All Cures is the UK's first full-service online pharmacy and it's genuinely very impressive. The site is stocked with everything you'd expect to find in your local branch of Boots, including over-the-counter medicine, beauty products, toiletries, alternative medicine, photographic services and even NHS and private prescriptions. Obviously if you want them to provide medicine prescribed by your GP you'll have to post the prescription to All Cures (it's a freepost address) to ensure that they get it right but, other than that, everything is available instantly online. The prices compare favourably with high street pharmacies, everything is very well presented and ordering is a doddle – hard to fault really. Love it.

■ The rest of the best

Boots www.boots.co.uk
The high street favourite may not have its act together when it comes to selling medicine online but they're doing pretty well with beauty products and skincare. Ok, so it can't compete with All Cures at the moment either on price or range of products but big companies have a habit of fighting back hard when they feel threatened and if you already shop at Boots, this is a much simpler way to do it. The site is a combination of shop and magazine with advice on health, beauty and parenting plus the opportunity to stock up on everything you need to make you look (and smell) better – you can even collect Advantage Card points if you're into that sort of thing.

Look Fantastic www.lookfantastic.com
While Boots have taken the clutter-free, pastel-coloured, design route, Look Fantastic is beautifully busy with plenty of exclamation marks and unbelievable offers. The big cosmetic names are all here, including Wella, Paul Mitchell and Aveda, some at impressive discounts of up to 60 per cent, and the Which? Web Trader logo will make your shopping less stressful. Bored with simply looking good? Maybe it's time to Look Fantastic.

My Nutrition www.mynutrition.co.uk

Back to the pastel colours (hurray!) with this award-winning 'on-line guide for everything to do with healthy food, eating and supplements'. The shopping area is only a very small part of what's on offer here with news, a free nutrition consultation and expert advice all thrown in for good measure. If you simply want to pick up some hand cream you'll probably prefer Boots or All Cures but if you're trying to live a healthy life, My Nutrition will set you off on the right track.

■ The best of the rest

Avon www.uk.avon.com

The whole Avon range is available on this easy-to-use, if slightly bland, site. There are some pretty reasonable discounts for ordering online.

Lush www.lush.co.uk

The UK's most fragrant beauty shop was revamping its site at the time of writing so there wasn't much to see. Their mail order service is superb though so if it's working again now – you can expect something pretty special.

Specialist shops

For general health and beauty purchases, you won't find much better than the internet's health and beauty superstores but if you have special requirements or need a little advice before you buy then you'll find plenty of specialist shops who are more than happy to take your money... er... sorry... questions.

■ *The best of the best*

Iris Online www.iris-online.co.uk

Iris Online provides a simple but very effective way to buy contact lenses without paying over the odds for them. Simply send them your lens prescription and they'll supply everything you need. There's not really much else to say – the site is well laid out, shopping is easy and the prices are great. Sorted.

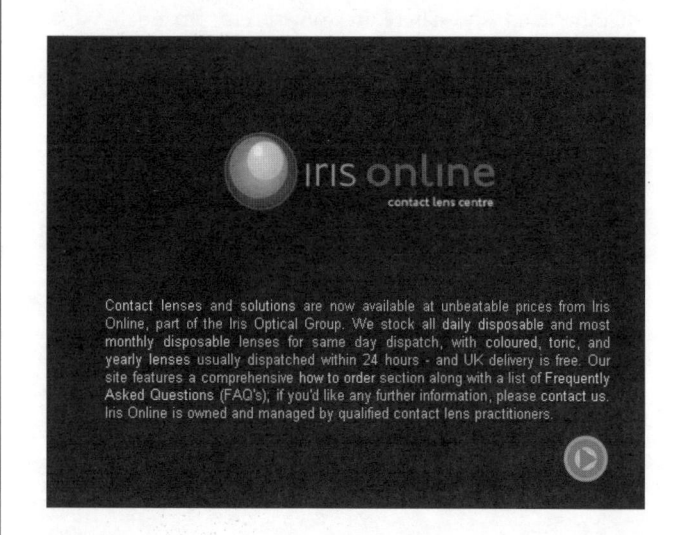

> iris online
> contact lens centre
>
> Contact lenses and solutions are now available at unbeatable prices from Iris Online, part of the Iris Optical Group. We stock all daily disposable and most monthly disposable lenses for same day dispatch, with coloured, toric, and yearly lenses usually dispatched within 24 hours - and UK delivery is free. Our site features a comprehensive how to order section along with a list of Frequently Asked Questions (FAQ's); if you'd like any further information, please contact us. Iris Online is owned and managed by qualified contact lens practitioners.

■ *The rest of the best*

Burgins Perfumery www.burginsperfumery.co.uk

The design may leave something to be desired but you can't fault the range of perfumes stocked by this York-based site. The site is separated into products for him and products for her all catalogued into alphabetical order – from Acqua di Gio to Zut. There's even gift wrapping available if you're feeling generous.

The English Shaving Company www.theenglishshavingcompany.co.uk

Go on, have a wild stab in the dark and guess at what you'll find here. Shaving need no longer be a chore with this impressive range of shaving accessories, shaving creams and aftershaves from some of the UK's most established names. The prices are far from cheap but, then again, what price shaving perfection?

Condomania www.condomania.co.uk

No more embarrassment in the chemist with this well-designed and well-stocked store. There's a wide range to choose from and all orders are dispatched in a plain wrapper to avoid knowing looks from the postman. Stop sniggering at the back.

■ *The best of the rest*

Perfume Directory www.perfumedirectory.co.uk

Another no-frills fragrance site, this time complete with photographs so you know what you're buying.

7

sports and outdoor

Lovers of the great outdoors may not fancy the idea of sitting in front of a computer for hours on end but if you can afford to take a few minutes break from gorge walking and white water rafting, you'll find some excellent sportswear and sporting goods suppliers online. The big names may have the off-line market sewn up but when it comes to the web, it's every shop for itself which usually means discounts all round. Game on!

Sporting equipment

If you're serious about your sport, you'll want to make sure you've got the best equipment and accessories but buying everything can be costly to say the least. As luck would have it, the world's biggest sports shop is at your fingertips in the form of the world wide web. From cricket bats to swimming goggles – it is all available if you know where to look… and knowing where to look is what we do best.

■ The best of the best

Newitts www.newitts.co.uk

Newitts, the UK's largest mail order supplier of sporting goods in the UK, have been around since 1902 and, if their excellent site is anything to go by, they'll be around for a good few years yet. All of the thousands of products are available to order and, using a simple but very effective navigation system, it couldn't be easier to find what you're looking for. Once you've completed your order, you'll want to return to check out the nifty penalty shoot-out game and to sign up to the Newitts newsletter. In a nutshell, if you're into sport, you need to get into Newitts. Splendid.

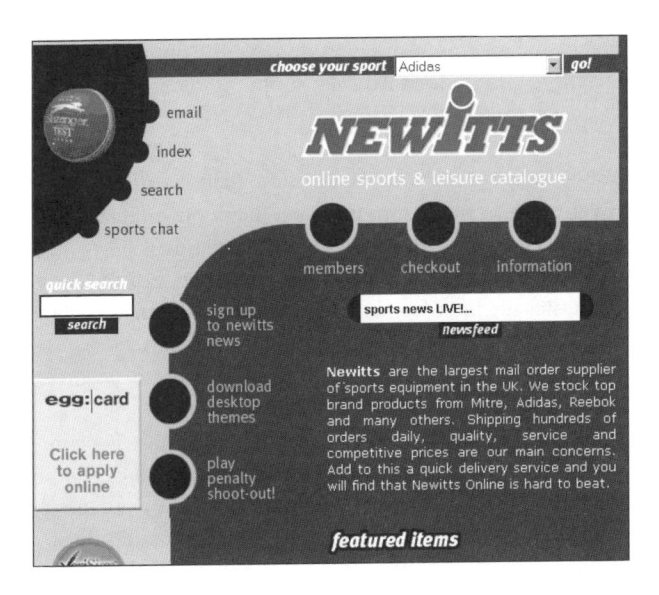

The rest of the best

Complete Outdoors www.complete-outdoors.co.uk

The name says it all. Shoes, bags, tents, walking poles and everything else you might need to get back to nature, all at down to earth prices. The design is a little basic and some more pictures of the products would help but if you know what you're looking for you shouldn't have too many problems. Postage isn't included though, so do check it out before you confirm your order.

Bid a Bike www.bidabike.com

Buying a bike is one thing but bidding for one? It may take some getting used to but specialist auction sites are growing in popularity. If you don't fancy the cut and thrust of the virtual auction room, you do have the option of using the more straightforward bike shopping section but, then again, where's the fun in that?

Legends Surf Shops www.legends-surf-shops.co.uk

If your idea of fun is standing on a plank of wood and getting wet, cold or bruised then you'll certainly want to surf over to Legends. All types of boards are featured here including surfboards and snowboards and if you're feeling creative you can even build your own skateboard.

Fishing Warehouse www.fishingwarehouse.co.uk

More than just an online shop, Fishing Warehouse is a complete portal for fishing enthusiasts. The site includes some extremely well-written articles plus a nice mix of news, reviews, forums and advice. Oh, and you can buy stuff too.

■ *The best of the rest*

Explorers Online www.explorers-online.com
Swiss Army knives, Ordinance survey maps, navigation tools and everything else you need to make it safely to the shops and back.

Simply Scuba www.simplyscuba.co.uk
Another self-explanatory name. Offers a wide range of diving equipment and all the clothing that goes with it.

Sportswear

Even if you're not particularly sporty, you can still make everyone think you are with the right clothes. Big-name brands like Nike and Reebok can usually be picked up cheaper from the stores in Chapter 5 Clothing and fashion but for everything else, you won't find better than our recommended sportswear stores.

■ *The best of the best*

Blacks www.blacks.co.uk
Blacks are already famous for offering sports and outdoor wear on the high street but, like so many before them, they've decided to take a leap on to the web. Unlike many before them, however, they've actually done a very good job of it, offering a complete range of hiking shoes, rucksacks and related outdoor wear in an easy-to-browse format. The prices may not be the cheapest in the business but the site looks great and products can be ordered online

(with free delivery) or picked up from your nearest high street branch.

■ *The rest of the best*

Discount Sports **www.discountsports.co.uk**
No matter whether you're seriously sporty or just want to look cool in summer, Discount Sports will have something to suit you. Trainers, T-shirts and other sportswear with free delivery and – you've guessed it – discounted prices. If you're not happy with a purchase, they'll send you a refund (minus postage) in the form of a credit note.

Kitbag www.kitbag.com

Kitbag started life by supplying replica football kits at internet prices but has since branched out into rugby, cricket and even Formula One clothing. Having been online for years, the company clearly knows how to sell on the web – ordering is a piece of cake and the after-sales service is not too shoddy either. WAP users will be pleased to hear that once you've signed up at the site you can shop instantly using a mobile phone so, no matter where you're playing, it's never been easier to get your kit on.

JD Sports www.jdsports.co.uk

You've seen them on the high street, now you can visit them online. As you'd expect, there's plenty of fashionable street and sportswear, including replica football kits and a good selection of trainers. Buying online could be easier and the prices aren't too amazing but if you're nervous about shopping online, an established name like JD Sports is a good place to start.

9 Feet www.9feet.com

Not only does 9 Feet look extremely impressive, it also obviously knows its stuff. Claiming to be 'as into the outdoors as you are' the site provides clothing and accessories for mountain biking, adventure sports, hiking, walking, climbing, cycling and everything else you can think of. Plenty of suitably exciting photography, a neat ordering system and competitive pricing make it well worth a visit.

Betting

If you don't fancy getting muddy and tired but still want to experience some sporting excitement then why not have a flutter on the horses… or the dogs… or the football… or the cricket… or just about anything you can possibly think of. Many of the bigger online betting shops are located offshore so you can enjoy a little tax-free gambling but if you do go for one of these make sure you know who you are dealing with otherwise the odds of getting anything back may be a lot worse than you expect. It goes without saying, these are for over-18s only. So there.

■ The best of the best

Sporting Bet www.sportingbet.com

The first thing to know about Sporting Bet is that it's tax free. No matter if you live in the UK, Australia, the US or even Finland you can place bets on some of the world's most high-profile sporting events, including football, basketball, hockey, soccer, cricket, motor sport, golf, horse racing, tennis and more. Once you've opened an account you can start betting straight away and, as a member of the British Betting Office Association, you can be pretty confident that Sporting Bet will look after your money.

■ The rest of the best

Blue Sq www.bluesq.com
Blue Sq(uare) is definitely one of the coolest online gambling sites and it's not all sport either. Although you can place a bet on the usual array of sporting competitions, it's much more fun to bet on US Presidential elections and the plot of your favourite soap. The layout is extremely fresh and funky and betting is as simple as you would expect.

Eurobet www.eurobet.co.uk
Betting giant Coral's foray into the world of e-commerce is predictably professional. Behind the uncluttered design lies an easy-to-use account application system allowing you to get up and running in no time and if you want to want to know a little bit more before you place a bet, Coral have provided plenty of reassuring information about themselves. A pretty safe bet.

8

home and garden

No matter whether you prefer to do it yourself or simply pick up the phone and call in the interior designers, you'll find no shortage of ideas for your home and garden. DIYers will want to head straight for Homebase (www.homebase.co.uk) or MFI's shrine to flat-pack furniture (www.mfi.co.uk) while budding Alan Titchmarshes will find a world of inspiration (and shrubs) at the likes of E-Garden (www.e-garden.co.uk). So don't let the grass grow beneath your feet – dig deep and home in on our favourite home and garden sites. There's no place like them.

Home improvement

Although the name of this section may be a little misleading as many of the home improvement stores do have a gardening section, we have tried to select the sites which specialise in interiors and furniture. Don't forget, of course, that many of the sites listed in Department stores and malls (see Chapter 2) also have plenty of home improvement bits and pieces.

■ The best of the best

Furniture Webstore www.furniturewebstore.co.uk

It may be slow loading at first but it's worth waiting those extra few seccond s for this superb furniture store. Specialising in beds, but with sofas and other stuff thrown in for good measure, they claim to be able to deliver a quality divan bed almost anywhere in the UK in less than 48 hours and even if time isn't that much of a problem you'll find plenty to choose from. UK delivery is free and the site supports the Which? Web Trader code of practice so you can sleep that little bit easier in your (new) bed.

■ The rest of the best

Cooksons www.cooksons.com

Ready-made furniture is one thing but if you really want to feel a sense of achievement, there's nothing like putting up a shelf or building a wall. Of course, you won't get too far without a decent set of tools and Cookson's have more than most – over 50,000 different hand and power tools are on offer all at extremely reasonable prices. Considering how many products there are to choose from, the site is surprisingly easy to navigate and ordering is a piece of cake – if only they didn't have that utterly pointless welcome page.

Space2 www.space2.com

If you work from home, you'll love this ultra-stylish range of home office furniture – exclusively designed and sold by Space2. The award-winning desks and workstations are designed to allow you to work comfortably and are durable enough to withstand the rigours of life at home but the great news is that, unlike their competitors, Space2 deliver within a couple of weeks so you can start working smarter almost straight away.

MFI www.mfi.co.uk

Bedrooms, kitchens and other little bits of self-assembly heaven make up this impressive-looking site from MFI. The range of furniture on offer could be a little better and, although there are a few special offers, the prices are pretty much what you'd expect in any of their Homeworks stores. In a nutshell, unless you know exactly what you're looking for, you'll still need to visit your local branch but if you do decide to order online it's very straightforward and everything will be delivered directly to your door.

Gardening

For some reason, gardening sites seem to be more of a growth (pun intended) area than other types of home improvement. We can only assume that people who spend hours online would rather relax outdoors than stay inside –

which can only be a good thing. If you have green fingers, or want to find someone who does, then spring over to some of the following top-notch garden sites.

■ The best of the best

Birstall www.birstall.co.uk

It's certainly not the sexiest-looking site on the web but as online garden centres go, Birstall takes some beating. From seeds to shrubs via trowels and trees, the site is easily as well stocked as your local garden centre but without the hassle of dragging the family around behind you. Ordering is 100% secure, delivery is suitably prompt and there's plenty of advice available if you need it. Definitely a site that deserves to do well.

■ The rest of the best

Dig It www.dig-it.co.uk

Dig It is one of the new breed of 'aren't plants cool' gardening sites which supply all of the usual gardening stuff but will also design and deliver a ready-made garden to your door – for a price. The design is certainly extremely hip with arty graphics and an easy-to-navigate shopping system but the range of products can't touch the likes of Birstall. As for the question of whether gardening can ever be truly cool… Dig It seems pretty convinced. We blame Charlie Dimmock.

E-Garden www.e-garden.co.uk

Hot on the heels of E-Bay, E-Trade, E-Shop et al. comes the creatively titled E-Garden. The main attraction is the stable of celebrity writers who contribute to the site's excellent advice areas but the shopping section is well worth a look with its selection of products and gardening books for beginners and professionals alike. Like Dig It, there is a certain amount of style over content but new gardeners will find plenty of interest.

■ *The best of the rest*

Conservatories Online www.conservatoriesonline.com

Thinking of buying a conservatory? This portal site is designed for you – just don't throw any stones.

Indian Ocean www.indian-ocean.co.uk

Extremely well-designed site offering the largest selection of teak furniture on the web.

9

food and drink

Whether you fancy a bar of chocolate or hunger for a gourmet meal, you'll be more than satisfied with the rich and varied selection of food and drink available on the web. Organic produce, fine wines, fresh fruit and all the rest of your weekly shopping can now be delivered directly to your door, leaving you even more time to slave over a hot stove. Or not.

Supermarkets

Posting a pork pie causes problems. This simple truth resulted in a slightly shaky start for online food and drink sales in the UK with companies struggling to arrange reliable and affordable methods of delivery. Obviously there are some products like hampers, cheese, chocolate and coffee which can be sent through the post or delivered by courier but sending your weekly shopping is not quite so easy. Fortunately, thanks largely to companies such as Iceland (www.iceland.co.uk) and Tesco (www.tesco.co.uk) British shoppers have taken in droves to the idea of having their shopping delivered, encouraging these companies (and more) to invest some serious money in rolling the service out nationwide. The non-city-dwellers amongst us may still have to rely on traditional supermarkets for a while yet but no matter where you live, it's never been easier to get stuffed.

The best of the best

Tesco www.tesco.co.uk

Tesco may not have delivery quite as sussed as Iceland but their range of products, customer service and ease of use are the best in the business. If you live within one of the growing number of Tesco delivery areas then it's simply a case of registering on the site, choosing your items and waiting for a shiny delivery van to arrive with your weekly shopping. Naturally you are going to get situations where something you order isn't in stock, in which case you get the chance to opt for an alternative product. It's not just about food and drink though – you can also buy books, music, gifts and even personal finance services. If this excellent service covered the whole of the UK there'd be no need to leave your house again. Well done Tesco.

■ The rest of the best

Iceland www.iceland.co.uk
Mum may have gone to Iceland in an old advertising campaign but thanks to Iceland's excellent home shopping service, she can stay home and put her feet up. An impressive range of groceries are available for delivery to an impressive 97% of the UK and as long as you spend over £40 you won't pay any extra for the service. When it comes to the number of products, Tesco and Sainsbury's are slightly better stocked but if you don't live in a major city – Iceland's home delivery is a godsend.

Sainsbury's www.sainsburys.co.uk
Like Tesco, Sainsbury's home delivery service is only available to those lucky people who live in a restricted delivery area but if you are fortunate enough to be eligible you can call upon the services of a team of specially trained shoppers to do your shopping for you. The site itself is very well thought out and there are some nice touches in the shopping system itself – such as allowing you to specify what size potatoes you want or how ripe you like your plums.

■ *The best of the rest*

Asda www.asda.co.uk
If Asda's web presence was the film *Twins* and Value mad is Arnold Schwarzenegger then their main information site is very definitely Danny DeVito. Functional but not superb.

Safeway www.safeway.co.uk
No online ordering yet but Safeway shoppers will enjoy the recipes, news and information on this extremely slick site.

Waitrose www.waitrose.com
Not as well stocked as the top dogs but the online ordering is well worth checking out if you usually shop at Waitrose.

Speciality food

Bored with beans? Tired of toast? If you're looking for a taste of the exotic, you'll find a wealth of speciality food shops waiting to take your order online. From organic food to fine wines, gourmet cheeses to smoked hams – it's all here. Tuck in.

■ *The best of the best*

Teddington Cheese www.teddingtoncheese.co.uk
When you feel cheesy there's only one place to come for over 130 varieties of the nation's favourite cracker topping. It's not just cheese though – crackers, chutneys and hampers are also available along with book offers and a free cheese-filled newsletter. Teddington Cheese may be a small company but its no-frills site is capable of taking on all

comers with its huge range, stress-free ordering and refreshingly friendly service. How cheese would want to be sold.

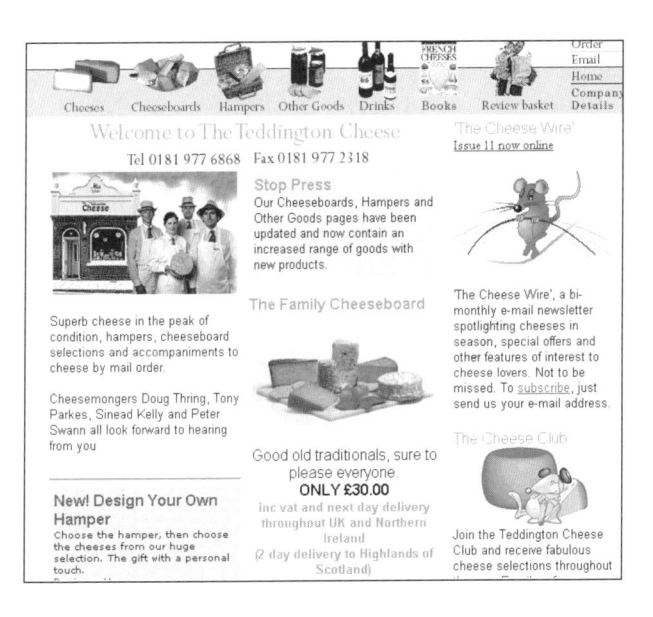

■ *The rest of the best*

Organics Direct www.organicsdirect.com

An award-winning and environmentally friendly site offering fruit, veg, pasta, baby food, bread, cakes and plenty more. The prices aren't cheap (although there's a 5% discount for regular orders) but you're buying into a set of ideals – everything is certified organic (and GM free), all of the growers are guaranteed a fair deal and the quality is second to none. Ordering is a little complicated but it's free if you buy enough. Excellent.

Clearwater Hampers www.hamper.com

If you prefer to buy your food by the basketful then this is definitely the site for you. Some extremely tasty-sounding hampers are available here packed with port, stilton, smoked salmon and other gourmet treats and if you can't find exactly what you're looking for you can even create your own. Ideal gifts for people who have everything. For more of the same try 800 Hampers (**www.800hampers.com**).

Fortnum and Mason www.fortnumandmason.co.uk

More hampers to be found here plus a nice range of chocolates, wine and gifts. The site may be user friendly but the prices are strictly for the well heeled. Expensive, but remember – you get what you pay for. Almost.

■ The best of the rest

Heinz Direct www.heinz-direct.co.uk

It may not be Fortnum and Mason but Heinz have done well with this tins by mail service. The delivery can take up to a month but if you don't mind waiting for your beans and baby food – it does the job.

Lobster www.lobster.co.uk

Luxury foods aplenty on this appropriately luxurious site. Caviar and champagne, fois gras and pastries and, surprise surprise, there's even a range of hampers. If you enjoy your food and don't mind paying a few quid for the best – that's what you'll get here.

Drink

Perhaps it's a question of profit or maybe internet users are all a bunch of boozers but it's much easier to buy alcohol online than it is to buy soft drinks. Oh well, if you can put up with the inconvenience of being forced to drink alcohol rather than mineral water you'll be spoilt for choice on our recommended virtual off-licences.

■ The best of the best

Chateau Online www.chateauonline.co.uk

Welcome to wine lovers' heaven. Chateau Online combines an excellent range of wine with expert advice from a top sommelier so you can be sure that you're getting the best, and with bases in France, Germany and Ireland as well as the UK site you're certainly not dealing with a fly-by-night operation. Even if you don't want to make a purchase, you'll find plenty to do on the site with forums and advice on how to set up a cellar and match the right food to the right wine. Ordering, as you've probably guessed, is simplicity itself and there's a flat-rate delivery charge of £5.99 so it's well worth stocking up.

■ *The rest of the best*

Last Orders www.lastorders.com

Ok, so Chateau Online may have the wine market sewn up but what if you fancy a beer? Last orders is the UK's leading online off-licence offering a massive range of beers, lagers, spirits, soft drinks and, yes, there's some wine too. The site is a joy to use with everything laid out in a logical order and the prices won't break the bank either. Although delivery is extremely prompt, it's a good idea to plan ahead if you're organising a weekend drinking session – if you order during the week you can take advantage of free delivery directly to your door. Very nice.

Amivin www.amivin.com

If over 4000 wines available for immediate delivery isn't enough to impress you then the range of extra features offered by Amivin certainly will be. Wine buffs will be pleased at how easy it is to navigate straight to a particular vintage but if you do need a little advice then Amivin's experts will be glad to point you in the right direction. There's also a number of excellent promotions, a gift wizard and a wine lovers' club. From everyday wines to the finest of the fine – you'll be spoilt for choice.

10

events and tickets

Sporting events, concerts, festivals, musicals and plays – whichever events you want to attend, you can save hours of queuing by booking your tickets on the web. There are plenty of companies offering to sort out your seats but the vast majority of tickets can be obtained through a small number of established online booking agents.

■ *The best of the best*

Ticketmaster www.ticketmaster.co.uk

Ticketmaster are already famous for selling tickets to the biggest and best UK events and attractions and their web version is no different. From athletics to the Farnborough Airshow and, of course, all the main shows and concerts – whatever live events you want to be a part of, it only takes a couple of clicks to reserve your tickets. It doesn't get much better than this.

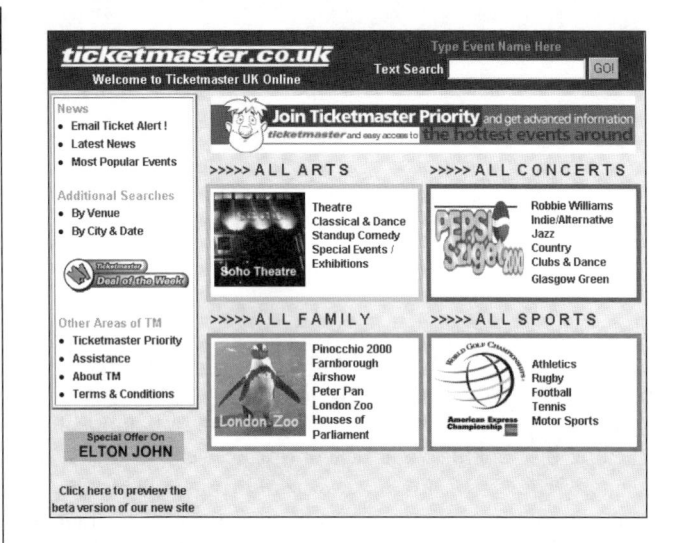

The rest of the best

Aloud www.aloud.com

Created by Emap Online, the people behind the superb A2B Travel (www.a2btravel.co.uk), you'd expect something pretty good from Aloud. Fortunately they haven't let us down with this excellent way of buying tickets to the UK's most popular live events. Simply type in the name of the artist, town or genre you're looking for and the booking engine will suggest possible events and dates. If you see something you like, it only takes a couple of clicks to make the booking. As with all ticket agents, you will pay a booking fee but when ordering is as painless as this it's well worth the extra pennies.

Ticketlinks **www.ticketlinks.co.uk**
Depending on your tastes this site is either far too cluttered or packed full of information. Either way you'll find tickets galore plus news, reviews and gossip about your favourite stories. Not quite as slick as the others but it does the job well.

■ The best of the rest

BBC Ticket Unit **www.bbc.co.uk/tickets**
Be in the studio audience for your favourite BBC shows. Just don't forget to applaud.

Odeon Cinemas **www.odeon.co.uk**
Excellent automated ticket booking for any Odeon cinema in the UK.

The Society of Ticket Agents and Resellers **www.s-t-a-r.org.uk**
If you can't find anywhere selling the tickets you want then it's worth trying STAR's members list for some alternatives.

travel

Travel has become one of the most popular uses of the internet and a huge number of sites have sprung up in the past couple of years to meet the growing demand for low-cost holidays, flights, accommodation and just about everything else. The difficult part is knowing which ones are worthy of your attention and which are just a waste of web space. For the full low-down on internet travel, check out Zingin's *The very best travel websites* or for some of the best starting points, read on.

Travel agents and portals

No matter what type of journey you're planning, your first stop should be one of the popular online travel agents or portal sites which will either allow you to book tickets directly or at least point you in the right direction.

Provided you stick with our suggested sites, making travel bookings online should be a risk-free affair but, for added peace of mind, you can make sure your chosen agent is a member of ABTA by visiting **www.abtanet.com**.

The best of the best

A2B Travel www.a2btravel.co.uk

No matter where, how or why you're travelling, don't leave home until you've checked out A2B Travel. A2B is the UK's largest travel information and booking portal. As it's designed by publishing giant EMAP, you'd expect excellent design and content but even by their normal standards this is something special. The layout may be a little cluttered for some tastes but it only reinforces how much information is packed into the site. Whether you prefer to travel by plane, train or Eurostar you'll find timetables, online booking and everything else you might need.

A2B have also put together a network of specialist sites which are designed to make your journey that little bit smoother. Check out A2B Airports (**www.a2bairports.com**),

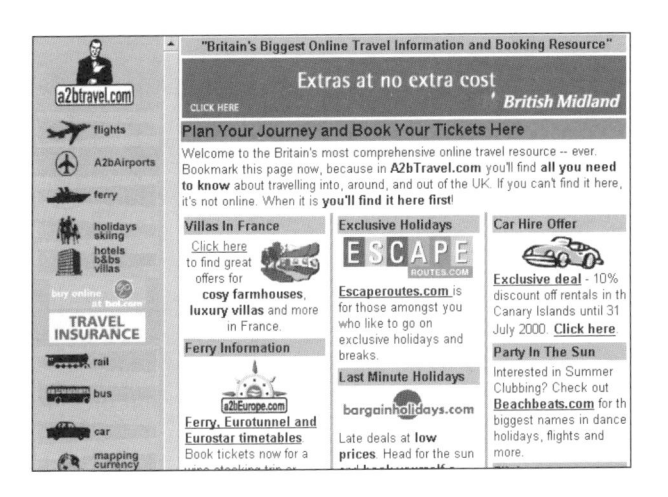

Escape Routes (www.escaperoutes.net) and A2B Europe (www.a2beurope.com) for starters.

■ The rest of the best

Travelocity www.travelocity.co.uk
While Travelocity does offer plenty of useful travel information, including some well-written destination guides, the site's main strength is its easy-to-use flight and hotel booking system. Behind the wonderfully cluttered front page you'll find a veritable goldmine of flights, hotel rooms, package holidays, weekend breaks and car hire. Tread carefully though, the prices offered are not always the cheapest available so it's worth checking Expedia (www.expedia.co.uk), Teletext (www.teletext.co.uk/holidays) and the rest to make sure you're getting the best deal.

Utravel www.utravel.co.uk
Utravel may be a relative newcomer to the online travel arena but it's quickly become a thoroughly decent alternative to the more established sites. Rather than focusing on one specific area of travel, you'll find everything from flights to ferries covered in more than acceptable detail. Admittedly most of the stuff here is done better by A2B but, as wannabes go, it's one of the best.

Expedia www.expedia.co.uk
The formula here is the same as the other travel sites with flights, accommodation and car hire but the real prize winner is their price comparison tool which lets you find the best deal on your holiday.

■ The best of the rest

Teletext www.teletext.co.uk/holidays
Teletext's holiday site offers some of the UK's lowest holiday prices – and you won't need to hunt for the remote control to find them.

Brochure Bank www.brochurebank.co.uk
Save yourself the hassle of traipsing around travel agents. These folk will deliver brochures from the UK's leading tour operators direct to your door – free of charge.

Specialist travel companies

So far we've concentrated on sites that provide a pretty general range travel services. There are, however, a growing number of operators who cater for specific areas of the market such as student travel, late bookings and the over-50s.

If you're just looking for a family holiday or a business flight then you're almost certainly better off with the mainstream companies but, if you're looking for tailor-made travel, look no further.

■ The best of the best

Last Minute www.lastminute.com
Specialising in impulse travel bookings rather than family package holidays, you'll find some rock-bottom prices on European travel and accommodation. If you're the sort of person who worries about every detail when making travel

arrangements then you might not feel entirely comfortable with this type of service as there's not much time to confirm your booking. If, on the other hand, you love to live life on the edge and/or on the cheap – make sure you leave it to the Last Minute.

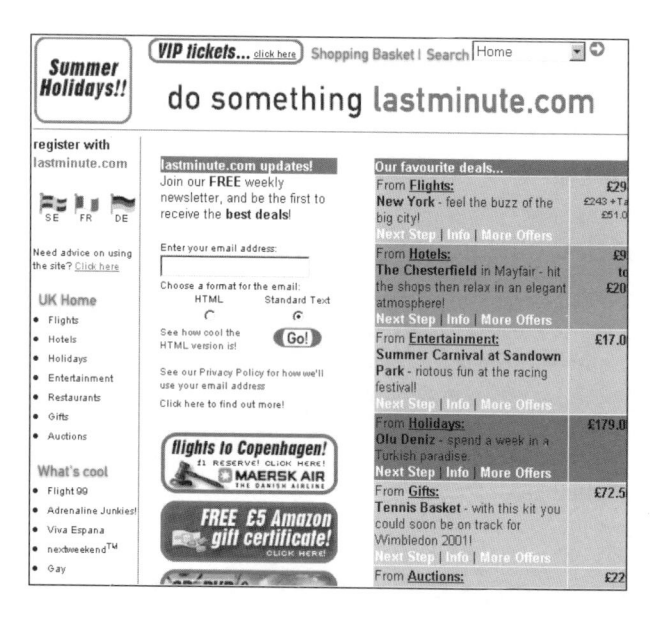

The rest of the best

STA Travel www.statravel.co.uk

Already a firm favourite with students, STA Travel has created a suitably fresh and funky site which offers low-cost flights, overland travel and insurance services. You can make an online booking or use the site to find your nearest branch – there's over 250 to choose from. For more of the same, also try Campus Travel (www.usitcampus.co.uk).

Board It www.boardit.com

Your one-stop shop for all things snowboardy. Make travel arrangements, find out the latest snowboarding news, browse the photo galleries and even check out a web cam of your chosen resort. A very well-put-together site which will appeal to beginners and pros alike. Skiers will want to hurtle towards 1Ski (www.1ski.co.uk).

Club 18-30 www.club18-30.co.uk

If you don't know about Club 18-30 holidays already, you probably wouldn't want to go on one. Sun, sea, sand and… so much more.

Saga www.saga.co.uk

Synonymous with high-quality over-50s travel, Saga offer holidays to pretty much anywhere on the planet. They've also recently branched out into insurance and other financial services.

12

toys and gifts

Young or old, everyone loves to receive presents and the internet is packed full of present ideas. Toys, games, gadgets, gizmos, flowers, chocolates, vouchers and more means there's something for everyone and, if you still can't find the ideal gift, don't forget to try the big Entertainment stores who usually offer gift wrapping and delivery services.

Toys and games

The fact that kids can't get hold of their own credit card means that the vast majority of toys bought online are intended as gifts. No matter whether you're looking for classic toys and games or the latest craze – the world's largest (virtual) toyshop is only a click away.

■ *The best of the best*

E-Toys **www.etoys.co.uk**
Unlike many of the other online toy stores, E-Toys seems to have realised that most people who buy toys online are in

fact adults. The site is designed to make it easy to browse by age range, brand or category and the range is certainly impressive – there's plenty of old favourites as well as the latest toys. A member of the Which? Web Trader scheme.

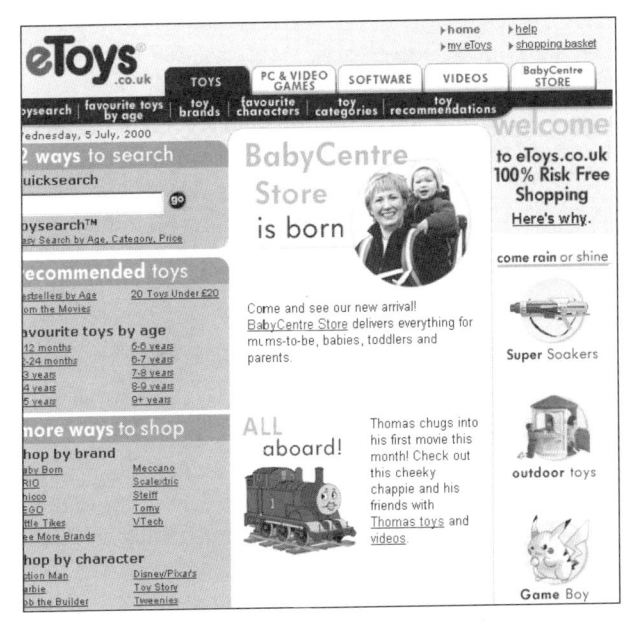

The rest of the best

Toyzone www.toyzone.co.uk

Toyzone take the opposite approach to E-Toys in that they've designed their site to be extremely appealing to kids. A colourful alien is on hand to show you around, there's a bulletin board and plenty of photos of the toys to show you what you're buying – all very nice but it doesn't make it any easier to actually spend money. Having said that, when you do manage to find what you need it's a simple enough process to place your order and delivery is not too sluggish either.

Early Learning Centre www.elc.co.uk
This suitably colourful but thoroughly uncluttered site is great if you're buying for younger children. All of the Early Learning favourites are available and you can search by ELC catalogue number if you already know what you're looking for. The site claims to be 'for moments money can't buy' but if you're determined to try to spend something then it's extremely easy to do owing to the excellent range and the silky smooth ordering system – and there's even order tracking to keep track of your toys' progress.

Toys 'R' Us www.toysrus.co.uk
Following a recent redesign, Geoffrey and the gang are really starting to make some progress online. A big chunk of their range is available for instant delivery, including (naturally) the latest toys and games and, thanks to a deal with Talking Shop (www.talkingshop.co.uk), you can even pick up a mobile phone on the site – ideal for today's connected youngsters. The design might not be anything special but, as they're quick to point out, Toys R Us are backed by a chain of bricks and mortar stores so you can order in total confidence.

Hamleys www.hamleys.com
It may well be the world's finest toy shop in the real world but on the internet Hamleys are not quite at the top of the

tree. The site is extremely professional looking and finding particular items shouldn't cause you too many problems. Unfortunately the site doesn't manage to achieve the parent friendliness of E-Toys or the fun and excitement of Toyzone so it's difficult to tell who Hamleys are targeting – with prices also in dollars perhaps they're hoping for some sales from across the pond? All in all, it's a good way to shop from Hamleys but not great if you're just doing some general toy shopping.

Gifts

It may be better to give than to receive but if you don't fancy trekking around the shops looking for the ideal gift you can save both time and money by doing your present buying online. If you want to cut out all the hassle some shops will even gift wrap your presents and send them straight to the recipient but if you choose to take that route, it's worth remembering the recent story of the Amazon (www.amazon.co.uk) customer who ordered a book to be sent straight to an elderly relative – unfortunately, owing to a mix-up by the world's largest bookstore the gentleman in question actually received a book full of erotic pictures. Doh.

■ *The best of the best*

Clare Florist www.clareflorist.co.uk
Saying it with flowers couldn't be simpler with this impressive site from the official florist to Edinburgh Castle. Each of the themed arrangements is illustrated with extremely clear photos and forgetful romantics will be relieved to hear

that if you order before 11a.m. you can take advantage of same-day delivery – or, if you miss the deadline, they'll guarantee next-day delivery. Clare Florist is one of those sites that we could rave about all day if you gave us the chance – but, to put it simply, if you're buying flowers this has to be your first stop. Blooming marvellous.

■ The rest of the best

Interflora www.interflora.co.uk

If you want to deliver flowers abroad then Interflora are the people to trust. With offices across the world from Algeria to Zambia, you won't have any problems reaching friends and family wherever they happen to be and Interflora's reputation means that you can be confident that the quality will be top notch. Gimmick lovers will be delighted with the site's personal reminder feature which promises that you'll never miss another occasion – or another opportunity to send flowers presumably.

Thorntons www.thorntons.co.uk
You already know the Thorntons product range – chocolate, fudge, toffee and assorted chewy things. Their slightly cluttered site is a great way to send your loved one a few extra calories and once you've spent a few minutes on the site you'll probably want to place an order for personal consumption as well. For those with entrepreneurial tendencies there's also information about setting up a Thorntons franchise. Tasty.

Art Republic www.artrepublic.com
It's not strictly speaking a gift site but, if you're buying for an art lover, you'll find a wealth of ideas at Art Republic. There are quality prints and posters a-plenty and if you can't find the image you're looking for you can e-mail their experienced team who will be more than happy to help you out.

■ The best of the rest

Voucher Express www.voucherexpress.co.uk
Ok, so gift vouchers may be the easy way out of present buying but if you're not sure what they'd like then you can't go far wrong. All of the big names in UK retail and restaurants are featured, including Our Price, PC World, Virgin, TGI Fridays and Victoria Wine, so you're bound to find something suitable but do watch out for the somewhat steep postage charges.

Balloon in a Box www.ballooninabox.co.uk
Show them you care with a balloon. In a box.

Gadgets

Having trouble buying a present for the person who has everything? Worry no longer. Ever since those innovation-packed magazines started falling out of Sunday papers gadgets have been growing in popularity. From the impressively useful ('how do they do it?') to the utterly useless ('why do they do it?'), there's plenty to choose from in our favourite online gadget shops.

■ The best of the best

Firebox www.firebox.com

Make sure you set a spending limit before you visit Firebox because once you've had a chance to browse their amazing range of gadgets, gizmos and assorted cool stuff you'll want to buy it all. Claiming to be 'where men shop' the site will probably also be happy to take money from female shoppers but there is definitely a lad's mag feel about the whole thing, especially in the bachelor pad essentials department.

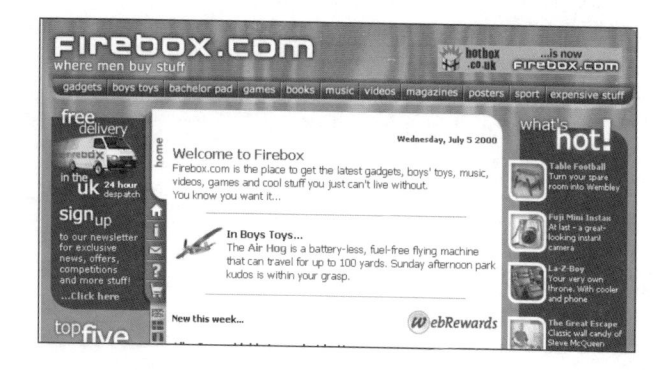

Look out for the La-Z-Boy chair as seen on Friends and the ultra-nifty indoor helium airship.

■ The rest of the best

Boys Stuff www.boysstuff.co.uk

The one-stop shop for big boys' toys doesn't quite achieve the same level of coolness but it's a pretty good bet if you can't find something suitable at Firebox. All the usual (and unusual) gadgets and gizmos are here, with a monthly rundown of the 9 hottest products to give you some ideas, and if you want to keep up with all the latest releases make sure you sign up to the site's free newsletter. Great stuff.

The Gadget Shop www.thegadgetshop.co.uk

The high street's favourite gadget emporium has recently revamped its web site (not before time) and is now a fully functioning, well-stocked, online store. Gadget Shop exclusives and old favourites are available for immediate (free) delivery and the money-back guarantee gives you no reason to endure the unfathomable queuing system of their real-world stores.

Alt Gifts www.alt-gifts.com

Alt(ernative) Gifts offers much more than just gadgets with a wide range of imaginative present ideas which are just perfect for the person who has everything. If you can't find anything suitable from their huge range of products (which includes everything from Italian design to comedy soap) then the Alt Gift experts are on hand to help you out and there are even electronic cards and a reminder service for when you've finished shopping.

13

classifieds and auctions

Buying what you want and selling what you don't has never been easier than on the electronic jumble sale that is internet classified and auction sites. If you have something to sell and you know exactly how much you want for it then sites such as Exchange and Mart (**www.exchangeandmart.co.uk**) and Preloved (**www.preloved.co.uk**) will allow you to advertise to millions of potential buyers – while also tempting you with a huge number of second-hand cars, furniture, computers and even (if you look hard enough) suits of armour. On the other hand, if you prefer the excitement of the auction room, you'll want to check out the likes of Ebay (**www.ebay. co.uk**) and Go Ricardo (**www.goricardo.co.uk**) – just make sure you know what you're bidding for before you part with your money.

Classifieds

Putting an advert in the local paper is *soooo* last century – especially when you consider the ease with which you can now reach millions of people on the web. Admittedly, some of the smaller classifieds sites don't get nearly enough traffic to bother with but if you stick to our selected few you will have that old moped out of your living room in no time. Of course, if you don't already have a moped in your living room and would like to get hold of one there are some excellent bargains to be had but remember – *caveat emptor*.

■ The best of the best

Loot www.loot.com

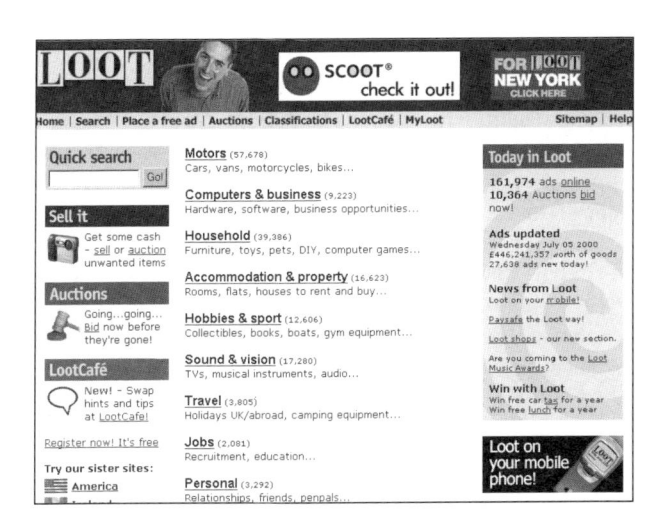

Hundreds of thousands of adverts and tens of thousands of auctions make Loot one of the best places to get rid of your old stuff and buy a whole load of new stuff. Advertising on the site is free and you can even access it using your WAP-enabled mobile phone so you won't miss out on the bargains no matter where you happen to be. Regular Looters will also want to grab a coffee in the virtual café which provides a forum for sellers and buyers to exchange tips and tricks. Very nice.

■ The rest of the best

Exchange and Mart www.exchangeandmart.co.uk

Getting around Exchange and Mart's online edition could be easier but the sheer number of daily visitors to the site and the fact that your ad will appear in the paper version makes it an essential destination, especially if you're selling your car. Placing an ad or contacting a seller is simple enough and there's also a live auction if you like that sort of thing.

Autotrader www.autotrader.co.uk

Autotrader, already the first choice for many a discerning car buyer, have established themselves firmly on the web with this extremely user-friendly buying and selling site. New and used cars, insurance services, finance and even an impressive news section make it child's play to find your perfect vehicle. For more of the same try Fish 4 Cars (**www.fish4cars.co.uk**).

Preloved www.preloved.co.uk

Preloved may not be the first name that springs to mind when you think of classifieds but this internet-only service is well designed, user friendly and certainly worth checking out if you're looking for a bargain.

Auction sites

Auctions are *the* major growth area in online trading and it seems that everyone is jumping on the bandwagon from Amazon (www.amazon.co.uk/auctions) to Yahoo! (uk.auctions.yahoo.com) but if you want to find the best bargains and the biggest number of buyers then make sure you check out some of our favourites.

■ The best of the best

Ebay www.ebay.co.uk

The UK branch of this huge global trading network is packed to the rafters with more items for sale than you could shake an auctioneer's hammer at. Putting an item up for sale or making a bid takes only a few clicks and Ebay automatically insure you against fraud so you can buy with confidence – just don't get too carried away with the beanie babies and signed celebrity photos.

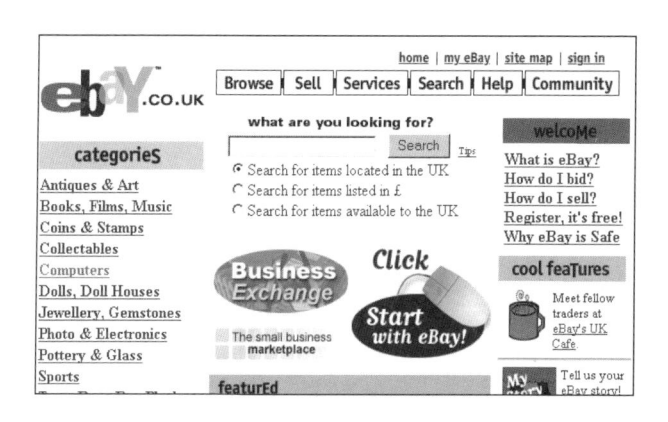

The rest of the best

QXL www.qxl.com

QXL are trying to position themselves as being slightly more upmarket than the likes of Ebay by offering online antique valuations and discounted hotel rooms through their site. The whole affair is certainly much slicker than some of the others but there are also fewer bargains to be had – if that's important to you. If you really want to bid on tickets, events and more exclusive items you'll also want to check out the excellent Fired Up (www.firedup.com).

Yahoo! Auctions uk.auctions.yahoo.com

Packed with bargains, wonderfully cluttered and so very Yahoo!-ish, this international auction site from the search giant features items from both the UK and abroad. The huge choice offered by such a global range is great on the one hand but on the other hand it's important to check where you're buying from or who you're selling to in order to avoid huge delivery charges and the chance of fraud. If you want to stay within the UK, check out the small but perfectly formed Ebid (www.ebid.co.uk).

Amazon Auctions www.amazon.co.uk/auctions

As you'd expect, Amazon's auction site has more than its fair share of books, music and film, including signed first editions, rare vinyl and all the *Starwars* memorabilia you could ever want. There is, however, much more to it than that. The book giant have teamed up with Sotheby's (sothebys.amazon.com) to cater for those with more expensive tastes and there are certainly some desirable lots to be had – if you're prepared to spend some serious money.

Go Ricardo www.goricardo.co.uk

A newcomer to the UK, but an established name in Europe, Go Ricardo is definitely one of the coolest of the auction sites. The range is not quite as good as the likes of Yahoo! and Ebay but it's definitely diverse with everything from antiques to belly button jewellery on offer. Well worth a look.

Still looking?

Although we've tried to cover the most useful and interesting online shopping resources we're not infallible (hard to believe but true!).

If you can't find the information you're looking for then why not visit us on the web? The Zingin Shopping Guide (**www.zingin.com/guide/shopping**) contains all of the shops listed here plus an up-to-date directory of the best new resources for online shopaholics.

Don't panic if you're still having no luck, just surf over to our Search Guide (**www.zingin.com/guide/search**) where our team of human search experts will try their hardest to help you out – and it won't cost you a penny!

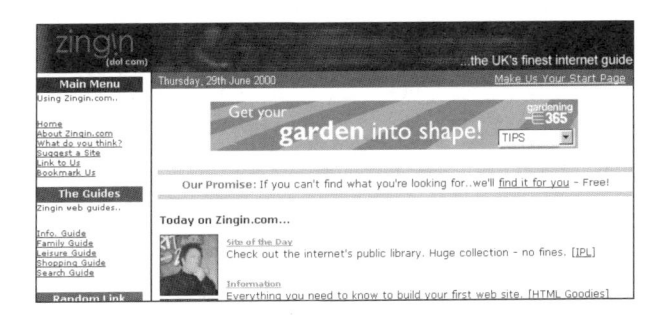

quick reference guide

Directories 12

2020 Shops	www.2020shops.com	14
Buy	www.buy.co.uk	16
Hoojit	www.hoojit.com	16
Kelkoo	www.kelkoo.com	13
Mondus	www.mondus.co.uk	15
My Taxi	www.mytaxi.co.uk	17
No Bags	www.nobags.com	17
Shopsmart	www.shopsmart.com	15
Shops on the Net	www.shopsonthenet.com	16
Value Mad	www.valuemad.co.uk	14
Y Bag	www.ybag.com	15

Department stores and malls 17

Argos	www.argos.co.uk	20
Barclay Square	www.barclaysquare.co.uk	19
Big Save	www.bigsave.com	19
Buckingham Gate	www.buckinghamgate.co.uk	20
Debenhams	www.debenhams.co.uk	17, 21
EshopOne	www.eshopone.co.uk	20
Great Universal	www.greatuniversal.co.uk	17
Marks and Spencer	www.marks-and-spencer.co.uk	21
QVC	www.qvc.co.uk	21
Shoppers Universe	www.shoppersuniverse.com	19

Entertainment superstores 22

Amazon	www.amazon.co.uk	22, 23
Jungle	www.jungle.com	24
Magazine Shop	www.magazineshop.co.uk	25
Streets Online	www.infront.co.uk	22, 24
WHSmith Online	www.whsmith.co.uk	24

Books 25

Alphabet Street	www.alphabetstreet.co.uk	24, 27
Basically Books	www.basicallybooks.co.uk	27
Bibliofind	www.bibliofind.com	28
BOL	www.uk.bol.com	26
Book Brain	www.bookbrain.co.uk	25
Booklovers	www.booklovers.co.uk	28
Online Originals	www.onlineoriginals.com	27
Waterstones Online	www.waterstones.co.uk	26

Music 28

101 CD	www.101cd.com	29
Audiostreet	www.audiostreet.co.uk	24, 28
Borrow Or Rob	www.borroworrob.com	31
Boxman	www.boxman.co.uk	30
CD Wow	www.cdwow.co.uk	31
Hard to Find	www.hard-to-find.co.uk	31
ICrunch	www.icrunch.com	32
Ministry of Sound	www.ministryofsound.co.uk	31
MP3.com	www.mp3.com	30
Music Match	www.musicmatch.com	30
PeopleSound	www.peoplesound.com	30
Replay	www.replay.co.uk	31
Sonique	www.sonique.com	30

Tower Europe	www.towereurope.com	32
Vitiminic	www.vitiminic.co.uk	31

Video and DVD 32

BBC Shop	www.bbcshop.com	34
Blackstar	www.blackstar.co.uk	32
Blockbuster	www.blockbuster.co.uk	34
DVD Street	www.dvdstreet.co.uk	24, 33
DVD World	www.dvdworld.co.uk	34
Film Store	www.filmstore.co.uk	35
Filmworld	www.filmworld.co.uk	33
MovieTrak	www.movietrak.com	34

Games 35

Gameplay	www.gameplay.com	37
Games Paradise	www.gamesparadise.com	37
Games Street	www.gamesstreet.co.uk	24, 36
Special Reserve	www.reserve.co.uk	37
UR Wired	www.urwired.com	35

Computer hardware 38

Apple	www.apple.com/uk	40
Dabs	www.dabs.com	42
Dell	www.dell.co.uk	40
Elonex	www.elonex.co.uk	41
Evesham	www.evesham.com	41
Gateway	www.gw2k.co.uk	41
Maplin	www.maplin.co.uk	42
Mesh	www.meshplc.co.uk	42
Micro Warehouse	www.microwarehouse.co.uk	40
PC World	www.pcworld.co.uk	39

Simply	www.simply.co.uk	42
Software Paradise	www.softwareparadise.co.uk	41
Viglen	www.viglen.co.uk	42

Electrical superstores 43

21 Store	www.21store.com	45
Battery Factory	www.batteryfactory.co.uk	46
Blue Spot	www.bluespot.co.uk	48
Comet	www.comet.co.uk	43
Dixons	www.dixons.co.uk	45
Easy Buy	www.easibuy.com	45
Hi-Fi Bitz	www.hifibitz.co.uk	47
Purley Radio	www.purleyradio.co.uk	47
Quality Electrical Direct	www.qed-uk.com	44
Richer Sounds	www.richersounds.co.uk	46
Techtronics	www.techtronics.com	48
Unbeatable	www.unbeatable.co.uk	43

Mobile phones 48

Beyond 2000	www.beyond-2000.co.uk	50
BT Cellnet	www.btcellnet.co.uk	51
Carphone Warehouse	www.carphonewarehouse.co.uk	48, 49
Miah Telecom	www.miah-telecom.co.uk	50
Orange	www.orange.co.uk	51
Phone Factory	www.phonefactory.com	50
Vodafone	www.vodafone-retail.co.uk	51

Clothing stores 52

AW Rust	www.awrust.co.uk	55
Best of British	www.thebestofbritish.com	55
Bumps Maternity	www.bumpsmaternity.com	56

Dressmart	www.dressmart.co.uk	54
Evans	www.evans.ltd.uk	56
Haburi	www.haburi.com	54
Into Fashion	www.intofashion.com	55
Kays	www.kaysnet.com	53
Novelty Togs	www.noveltytogs.com	56
Swerve	www.swerve.co.uk	55
Topman	www.topman.co.uk	54
Zoom	www.zoom.co.uk	53

Top brands 56

Diesel	www.diesel.co.uk	57
Fat Face	www.fatface.co.uk	56
La Redoute	www.redoute.co.uk	58
Skim	www.skim.com	58

Shoes and accessories 58

Accessorize	www.accessorize.co.uk	60
Agent Provocateur	www.agentprovocateur.com	61
Ann Summers	www.annsummers.co.uk	61
Brief Look	www.brieflook.co.uk	61
Cruelty Free Shop	www.crueltyfreeshop.com	61
Easy Shop	www.easyshop.co.uk	60
Marcus Shoes	www.marcusshoes.com	61
Shoe Shop	www.shoe-shop.com	59
Shoe World	www.shoeworld.com	59
Smart Bras	www.smartbras.com	61

Health and beauty superstores 62

All Cures	www.allcures.com	62, 63
Avon	www.uk.avon.com	65

Boots	www.boots.co.uk	62, 64
Look Fantastic	www.lookfantastic.com	64
Lush	www.lush.co.uk	65
My Nutrition	www.mynutrition.co.uk	65

Specialist health and beauty shops 65

Burgins Perfumery	www.burginsperfumery.co.uk	67
Condomania	www.condomania.co.uk	67
English Shaving Co.	www.theenglishshavingcompany.co.uk	67
Iris Online	www.iris-online.co.uk	66
Perfume Directory	www.perfumedirectory.co.uk	67

Sporting equipment 68

Bid a Bike	www.bidabike.com	70
Complete Outdoors	www.complete-outdoors.co.uk	70
Explorers Online	www.explorers-online.com	71
Fishing Warehouse	www.fishingwarehouse.co.uk	70
Legends Surf Shops	www.legends-surf-shops.co.uk	70
Newitts	www.newitts.co.uk	69
Simply Scuba	www.simplyscuba.co.uk	71

Sportswear 71

9 Feet	www.9feet.com	73
Blacks	www.blacks.co.uk	71
Discount Sports	www.discountsports.co.uk	72
JD Sports	www.jdsports.co.uk	73
Kitbag	www.kitbag.com	73

Betting 74

Blue Sq	www.bluesq.com	75

Eurobet www.eurobet.co.uk 75
Sporting Bet www.sportingbet.com 74

Home and garden 76

Cooksons	www.cooksons.com	77
Furniture Webstore	www.furniturewebstore.co.uk	77
Homebase	www.homebase.co.uk	76
MFI	www.mfi.co.uk	76, 78
Space2	www.space2.com	78

Gardening 78

Birstall	www.birstall.co.uk	79
Conservatories Online	www.conservatoriesonline.com	80
Dig It	www.dig-it.co.uk	79
E-Garden	www.e-garden.co.uk	80
Indian Ocean	www.indian-ocean.co.uk	80

Supermarkets 81

Asda	www.asda.co.uk	84
Iceland	www.iceland.co.uk	81, 83
Safeway	www.safeway.co.uk	84
Sainsbury's	www.sainsburys.co.uk	83
Tesco	www.tesco.co.uk	81, 82
Waitrose	www.waitrose.com	84

Speciality food 84

800 Hampers	www.800hampers.com	86
Clearwater Hampers	www.hamper.com	86
Fortnum and Mason	www.fortnumandmason.co.uk	86
Heinz Direct	www.heinz-direct.co.uk	86
Lobster	www.lobster.co.uk	86

| Organics Direct | www.organicsdirect.com 85 |
| Teddington Cheese | www.teddingtoncheese.co.uk 84 |

Drink 87

Amivin	www.amivin.com 88
Chateau Online	www.chateauonline.co.uk 87
Last Orders	www.lastorders.com 88

Events and tickets 89

Aloud	www.aloud.com 90
BBC Ticket Unit	www.bbc.co.uk/tickets 91
Odeon Cinemas	www.odeon.co.uk 91
S.T.A.R	www.s-t-a-r.org.uk 91
Ticketlinks	www.ticketlinks.co.uk 91
Ticketmaster	www.ticketmaster.co.uk 89

Travel agents and portals 92

A2B Airports	www.a2bairports.com 93
A2B Europe	www.a2beurope.com 94
A2B Travel	www.a2btravel.co.uk 93
ABTA	www.abtanet.com 92
Brochure Bank	www.brochurebank.co.uk 95
Escape Routes	www.escaperoutes.net 94
Expedia	www.expedia.co.uk 94
Teletext	www.teletext.co.uk/holidays 94, 95
Travelocity	www.travelocity.co.uk 94
Utravel	www.utravel.co.uk 94

Specialist travel companies 95

| 1Ski | www.1ski.co.uk 97 |
| Board It | www.boardit.com 97 |

Campus Travel   www.usitcampus.co.uk 97
Club 18-30   www.club18-30.co.uk 97
Last Minute   www.lastminute.com 95
Saga   www.saga.co.uk 97
STA Travel   www.statravel.co.uk 96

Toys and games 98

Early Learning Centre   www.elc.co.uk 100
E-Toys   www.etoys.co.uk 98
Hamleys   www.hamleys.com 100
Talking Shop   www.talkingshop.co.uk 100
Toys 'R' Us   www.toysrus.co.uk 100
Toyzone   www.toyzone.co.uk 99

Gifts 101

Art Rebublic   www.artrepublic.com 103
Balloon in a Box   www.ballooninabox.co.uk 103
Clare Florist   www.clareflorist.co.uk 101
Interflora   www.interflora.co.uk 102
Thorntons   www.thorntons.co.uk 103
Voucher Express   www.voucherexpress.co.uk 103

Gadgets 104

Alt Gifts   www.alt-gifts.com 105
Boys Stuff   www.boysstuff.co.uk 105
Firebox   www.firebox.com 104
The Gadget Shop   www.thegadgetshop.co.uk 105

Classifieds 106

Autotrader   www.autotrader.co.uk 108

Exchange and Mart	www.exchangeandmart.co.uk	106, 108
Fish 4 Cars	www.fish4cars.co.uk	108
Loot	www.loot.com	107
Preloved	www.preloved.co.uk	106, 108

Auction sites 109

Amazon Auctions	www.amazon.co.uk/auctions	109, 110
Ebay	www.ebay.co.uk	109
Ebid	www.ebid.co.uk	110
Fired Up	www.firedup.com	110
Go Ricardo	www.goricardo.co.uk	106, 111
QXL	www.qxl.com	110
Sotheby's	sothebys.amazon.com	110
Yahoo! Auctions	uk.auctions.yahoo.com	110

Zingin links

Feedback (E-mail)	feedback@zingin.com
Feedback (Form)	www.zingin.com/feedback.html
Home	www.zingin.com
Search Guide	www.zingin.com/guide/search
Suggest a Site	www.zingin.com/add.html
Shopping Guide	www.zingin.com/guide/shopping